Brittany

by Lindsay Hunt

After a year living and working in Spain,
Lindsay Hunt became a travel writer. Since
then, she has been a regular contributor
to a consumer magazine and has written a
number of hotel and destination guides. She
has spent time in many parts of France, and
has paced the length and breadth of Rivieran
strands, clambered up innumerable Parisian
hotel staircases and travelled round
Burgundy's vineyards on a bicycle

D1434182

AA Publishing

Above: *Poignant war memorial on Fouesnant's church*

Written by Lindsay Hunt
Updated by Lyn Parry

First published 2003
Reprinted Jan 2004. Reprinted May 2004.
This edition 2005. Information verified and updated.

© Automobile Association Developments Limited 2003, 2005

Published by AA Publishing, a trading name of Automobile Association Developments Limited, whose registered office is Southwood East, Apollo Rise, Farnborough, Hampshire GU14 0JW.
Registered number 1878835.

Find out more about AA Publishing and the wide range of travel publications and services the AA provides by visiting our website at www.theAA.com/bookshop

A01990

Colour separation: Keenes, Andover
Printed and bound in Italy by Printer Trento S.r.l.

Contents

About this Book 4

About this Book

This book is divided into five sections to cover the most important aspects of your visit to Brittany.

Viewing Brittany pages 5–14
An introduction to Brittany by the author
   Brittany's Features
   Essence of Brittany
   The Shaping of Brittany
   Peace and Quiet
   Brittany's Famous

Top Ten pages 15–26
The author's choice of the Top Ten places to see in Brittany, listed in alphabetical order, each with practical information.

What to See pages 27–90
An extensive guide to Brittany, with a brief introduction and an alphabetical listing of the main attractions
   Practical information
   Snippets of 'Did you know...' information
   5 suggested walks and 4 suggested drives
   2 features

Where To... pages 91–116
Detailed listings of the best places to eat, stay, shop, take the children and be entertained.

Practical Matters pages 117–124
A highly visual section containing essential travel information.

Maps
All map references are to the individual maps found in the What to See section of this guide.
For example, Dinan has the reference
✚ 29E4 – indicating the page on which the map is located and the grid square in which the town is to be found. A list of the maps that have been used in this travel guide can be found in the index.

Prices
Where appropriate, an indication of the cost of an establishment is given by € signs:

€€€ denotes higher prices, €€ denotes average prices, while € denotes lower charges.

Star Ratings
Most of the places described in this book have been given a separate rating:
✪✪✪   Do not miss
✪✪   Highly recommended
✪   Worth seeing

Viewing
Brittany

Above: *Pointe du Décollé*
Right: *Traditional Breton lace* coiffe

Lindsay Hunt's Brittany

Granite
Breton granite, the region's principal building stone, takes many forms. Spot it in prehistoric menhirs and megaliths, in lichen-blotched churches and calvaries, borderland fortresses, whitewashed holiday homes, even on luxury bathroom walls. Spectacular natural formations can be seen around the Côte de Granit Rose, eroded into weirdly organic shapes. Kersanton stone, malleable and more easily worked, was the medium of choice for monumental art in Brittany's many churches.

Pointe du Raz, one of Finistère's most dramatic headlands

The sea dominates this ragged, northwestern peninsula, and if you love that as much as I do, Brittany is an exhilarating destination. Brittany has as much coastline intricately fretted into its capes, bays, reefs, rocks, estuaries and islets as the whole of the rest of France together. For the Celtic tribes who first settled here during the Iron Age, Brittany was *Armor* – the Land by the Sea. Since then, generations of Bretons have earned a living from seafaring, from the Gaulish *Veneti* in their tin-laden sailing ships, through centuries of intrepid explorers, merchant adventurers, fishermen, corsairs and naval recruits. Today, the waves cast up new sources of revenue in the ferry terminals of Roscoff and St-Malo as thousands of British and Irish visitors converge on Brittany for the perfect seaside holiday – especially walking, boating and birdwatching.

The verdant Emerald Coast around St-Malo, the strangely eroded russet rocks of the Pink Granite Coast further west, and the lush, wooded estuaries of Cornouaille are some of the most charismatic stretches. Finistère's deadly reefs lie half-submerged like slumbering crocodiles, waiting for Atlantic storms, treacherous currents or bewildering sea-fogs to serve up their prey. Disasters still occur, despite the chain of lighthouses and hazard markers that studs this coast. The main feature of Morbihan's coastline is the huge tidal lagoon called the Golfe du Morbihan, scattered with hundreds of islets. Loire-Atlantique's low-lying shores boast the biggest, and some claim, Europe's most beautiful beach at La Baule.

Brittany offers far more than its magnificently varied seaside. It would be a pity to miss at least some of its interior, where medieval castles and mysterious standing stones await discovery. So do dozens of historic churches and those uniquely Breton architectural treasures, the elaborate parish closes and calvaries of central Finistère. It's a seasonal place, and not much happens in the winter months, but between Easter and October there's a continual round of festivals and happenings, many based on the Celtic culture that makes this region so vibrantly distinct from other parts of France.

Brittany's Features

Geography
• Maximum extent: around 200km from east to west.
• 1,800km of coastline, parts with a 50m tidal range (highest in France).
• 20,000km of rivers and streams, including over 600km of navigable waterways.
• 5,000km of bridleways and footpaths, including three of France's long-distance *Grandes Randonnées*.
• Two Regional Parks: Armorique – 172,000ha of land and ocean, including the Monts d'Arrée, the dramatic Crozon peninsula and the reef-strewn archipelagos of Ouessant and Sein;
La Brière – 40,000ha of peat-marsh once submerged below the sea.
• Regions: Haute-Bretagne (Upper Brittany near the eastern Marches) and Basse-Bretagne (Lower Brittany to the west).
• Highest altitude: 384m (Tuchen Gador, Monts d'Arrée).

Administration
• Since 1973, the *département* of Loire-Atlantique has officially formed part of the Pays-de-la-Loire region, but culturally still considers itself to be Breton.
• The other four *départements* are Ille-et-Vilaine, Côtes d'Armor, Finistère and Morbihan.

Economy
• About 60 per cent of Brittany's land is under cultivation, and is one of France's most productive agricultural regions.
• Dairy, poultry and pig-farming are important, but Brittany is especially renowned for market garden produce (over a million tons annually of artichokes, potatoes, cabbages, cauliflowers, peas, beans, salad crops, apples, straw-berries etc).
• Despite dwindling fish stocks and EU quota systems, the fishing industry is a vital mainstay of Breton ports like Le Guilvinec, Douarnenez, Concarneau and Audierne.
• Tourism is one of the region's biggest earners. Brittany is France's second most popular holiday area.
• Car manufacture and light engineering (electronics, computing, telecommunications) now supersede Brittany's declining shipbuilding and steel industries.
• Major ferry ports: St-Malo, Roscoff.
• Regional newspaper: *Ouest-France*, based in Rennes.

Seaweed
Seaweed is an increasingly important crop in Brittany. Harvested on an industrial scale, it is processed for a great variety of new uses besides being a time-honoured method of improving coastal soils. Culinary, pharmaceutical, cosmetic and therapeutic products are now on sale all over Brittany, especially at thalassotherapy centres like Roscoff and La Baule.

Newly harvested fields stretch into the distance on the flat reclaimed polders around Dol-de-Bretagne

Essence of Brittany

Above: *Lace* coiffe
Inset: *Artichoke*
Below: *Fishing boats at St-Malo*

As you head westwards, the Celtic ambience of Basse-Bretagne (Finistére) becomes more pronounced. It is here you may still hear the Breton language spoken, and even see a few traditional costumes worn at *pardons* and festivals. Church architecture takes on its idiosyncratic Breton form in the *enclos paroissial* (parish close). In rural areas, the population is still devoutly Catholic. Folk music, however, provides the most active sign of a revival in Breton culture. In the east, Haute-Bretagne slowly merges with the culture of its Norman neighbours and the more Gallic parts of France beyond the Loire.

THE **10** ESSENTIALS

If you only have a short time to visit Brittany, or would like to get a really complete picture of the region, here are the essentials:

• **Eat pancakes** A savoury *galette* (made with buckwheat flour) followed by a sweet, lacy *crêpe* makes a quick, inexpensive, filling meal. You'll find *crêperies* all over Brittany, though by no means all have mastered this exacting art form.

• **Visit some parish closes** These unique sights are mostly clustered around the Armorique Regional Park, and date from the 16th and 17th centuries when new-found prosperity was lavished on the village churches and the cemeteries surrounding them.

• **Order an *assiette de fruits de mer*** Whether oysters, scallops, mussels or langoustines are your favoured seafood, don't leave Brittany without trying one of these awesome platters, often served on beds of seaweed with big chunks of lemon.

• **Head for the coastal extremities** Brittany's westerly capes (Crozon, Sizun and Penmarc'h) and islands are especially dramatic during a gale, but the scenery is always stunning, especially along some of the old coastal watchpaths (*sentiers des douaniers*).

• **Take a boat-trip** Brittany is perfect for boating and there's a wonderful choice of river cruises, island hops and trips along the inland waterways. Take your camera and binoculars to watch birds and seals.

• **Try a typical Breton cake or pudding** A *kouign aman* (a sugary almond cake) or *far breton* (an eggy flan with prunes or raisins) will stoke up your energy levels. Local *pâtisseries* and specialist shops sell a bewildering variety of Breton biscuits too (packed in attractive tins, they make great presents to take home).

Left: *Bounty from the sea*

• **Track down some megaliths** Carnac has the best-known concentration of standing stones in Brittany, but dolmens, menhirs and cairns are sprinkled all over the region in quiet fields.

• **Experience a *criée*** Brittany's bustling fish auctions can be visited in a number of ports – but you'll have to get up early to see anything happening. Ask the local tourist office.

Below: *Paddling at Beg-Meil beach*

• **Test the beaches** Whatever else you do in Brittany, spend time on its glorious beaches. Scrubbed clean by some of the highest tides in Europe, many have EU Blue Flag status. Some are dangerous – heed flags and warning signs.

• **Look out for festivals** Most communities hold a festival or two during the year. Some are major cultural events attracting visitors from far and wide, but village saints' days and *pardons* can be just as memorable and often more genuinely typical of Breton life.

Even the young are proud of their traditional costume

9

The Shaping of Brittany

Left: *Cairn de Barnenez*
Right: *The Breton flag*

Duke of Brittany.

1303
St Yves, Brittany's famous lawyer saint, dies in Tréguier.

1346
The Hundred Years' War begins between France and England. Bertrand Du Guesclin's glorious military career takes off.

1351
The Battle of the Thirty takes place in Josselin.

1364
The De Montforts eventually triumph in the War of Succession for the Duchy of Brittany.

1491
The Duchess Anne becomes Queen of France for the first time.

1514
Anne dies.

1532
Brittany becomes a part of France under the Treaty of Vannes.

1534
Jacques Cartier sets out for the Northwest Passage, and discovers Canada.

1598
The Edict of Nantes ends

The mists of antiquity–8000 BC
Evidence of some of the world's earliest structured human settlements are found in Brittany. After the last Ice Age, hunter-gathering communities slowly re-establish themselves.

4500–1800 BC
The mysterious *alignements* of Carnac are built, but no one knows why.

1800–600 BC
The Bronze Age Bell-Beaker folk arrive, showing great artistry in ceramics, weaponry and gold jewellery.

***c* 600 BC**
Celtic peoples arrive sporadically over several centuries, gradually assimilating with the indigenous population and forming five recognisable tribes. Farmers, warriors and seafarers, they trade

Armorica's tin over great distances.

56 BC
Julius Caesar defeats the *Veneti* and completes his conquest of Gaul. Roman occupation brings centuries of peace.

5th–6th century AD
The fall of the Roman empire causes instability throughout Europe. Refugees flee western Britain after invasions of Vikings, Angles and Saxons, landing in Armorica and renaming it after their homeland – Brittany (Little Britain). Monks bring Christianity with them.

799
Frankish control is established over Brittany under a governor and protegé of Charlemagne, Nominoë.

845
Nominoë expels the Franks and becomes first

the Wars of
Religion.

1675
The Stamped
Paper Revolt –
a protest at
Louis XIV's
usurous
taxation to
finance his
extravagant
lifestyle.

1722
The Great Fire of Rennes
destroys a large part of
the old city.

1795
The royalist Chouans
stage an insurrection
against the excesses of
the Revolution.

1836
The Nantes–Brest Canal
is inaugurated.

1888
Gauguin visits Pont-Aven.

1896
The *Drummond Castle*
founders off Finistère,
causing great loss of life.

1914–1918
The Great War kills over
250,000 Breton citizens,
the heaviest losses
experienced anywhere in
relation to the population.

1923
The black-and-white
Breton flag is designed,
spearheading a wave of
separatist feeling and
extremist nationalism.

1939–1945
The men of Sein all
volunteer to
join De Gaulle's Free
French forces based in
England. Breton
Resistance groups help
many Allied service-men
to escape from occupied
France. Brittany suffers
massive casualties and
destruction of its
strategic ports.

1960s
The Artichoke Wars.
Farmers protest at falling
prices by dumping
surplus produce in the
streets of Paris.

1962
The radar station at
Pleumeur-Bodou
transmits and receives
the first transatlantic satellite broadcast via *Telstar*.

1967
Inauguration of the Rance
tidal barrage near Dinard.

1973
Alexis Gourvennec
begins a ferry service to
the UK, which eventually
becomes Brittany Ferries.
In a bureaucratic
redrawing of the map,
Loire-Atlantique is
severed from Brittany to
become part of Pays-de-
la-Loire.

1978
The *Amoco
Cadiz*
founders off
the Breton
coast and
spills oil into
the sea,
causing huge
pollution and the
death of many seabirds.

1987
A hurricane causes great
damage to Brittany's
ancient woodlands in the
Argoat.

1988
The Brest Charter is
implemented to encou-
rage regional investment
and urban regeneration.

1994
In a fishing protest, the
Breton Parliament
building in Rennes is
accidentally set on fire
and badly damaged.

1999
The tanker *Erika* causes
yet more oil pollution off
the Breton coast.

2002
Breton-born right-wing
extremist Jean-Marie Le
Pen wins unexpected
support in national
elections, defeating the
Socialists in the first ballot.

2004
The construction of
Queen Mary 2 is finished
at St-Nazaire.

11

Peace & Quiet

Though Brittany has little true wilderness and no high mountains, there are many wild places and a great range of different habitats. Many nature reserves have been set up to conserve its native flora and fauna. Two regional nature parks foster the social fabric of local communities as well as protecting the environment. Each of Brittany's *départements* offers something different in terms of scenery and species. Interpretative centres and *ecomusées* make useful starting points for learning about the area, and some provide escorted walks or tours.

If you prefer to explore alone, follow some of Brittany's waymarked trails. Three long-distance footpaths marked with red and white beacons traverse the region (GR34 leads along the north coast, GR38 runs through the Armorique Regional Nature Park and the Monts d'Arrée, and the GR37 follows the Nantes–Brest Canal). Countless shorter routes include coastal watchpaths (*sentiers des douaniers*), canal towpaths (*chemins de halage*), forest trails, pilgrimage routes and local rambles. Any tourist office can provide suggestions for self-guided walks and tours. Interesting themed routes enable you to retrace the footsteps of artists along the Emerald Coast, for instance, follow medieval pilgrims around cathedrals and shrines, or explore the lighthouses of western Finistère.

Twin lighthouses guard the rocks at Pointe de St-Mathieu

Armor (the coast)

Brittany's long, indented coastline and its countless offshore islands are havens for marine wildlife of many kinds. Seabird sanctuaries can be found at Cap Fréhel, Cap Sizun, Belle-Ile, Audierne and Les Sept-Iles (where puffins breed). Late spring and autumn are generally the most interesting times to see them, though there may be certain restrictions on visiting during the nesting season. In winter the Golfe du Morbihan plays host to a huge variety of migrant species. A glass-bottomed boat operates from Le Conquet, giving visitors a chance to observe the rich sea-life in Armorique's marine park, particularly grey seals and dolphins. Salt-tolerant plants colonise Brittany's exposed headlands and clifftops, particularly sea-pinks (thrift) and spring squills.

Argoat (the countryside)

The ancient forests that once cloaked the Breton countryside have mostly disappeared now, cleared for farmland or used as fuel and ship timber. Much was smashed to matchwood within minutes by the great hurricane of 1987, to be steadily replaced by a new habitat of low scrub and moorland. But tantalising fragments of the original great oak- and beech-woods still remain around Paimpont and Huelgoat, wreathed in Arthurian legends and full of wildlife. The Redon area is famed for its sweet chestnut forests. These woodlands give a glimpse of what Brittany must have looked like in earlier centuries.

View from Pointe du Grouin (top) where wildflowers grow in profusion among the rocks (above)

Elsewhere, lonely moorland covers much of inland Morbihan and Ille-et-Vilaine, and huge expanses of heather and moor grass can be found in the Armorique Regional Nature Park too, especially on the uplands of the Monts d'Arrée. Songbirds nest in the scrubland vegetation, and birds of prey soar overhead. Mushrooms and wild berries make tempting autumn pickings. Gorse is perhaps the most ubiquitous and striking plant species, flowering sporadically for most of the year, but a blaze of gold in late spring – the *ajoncs d'or* celebrated in local festivals. Loire-Atlantique's Grande Brière peat-bog is a haunting scene, where herons and egrets paddle through saltmarsh samphire, and bitterns boom in the reedbeds.

13

Brittany's Famous

Shapers of History

The great medieval warrior Bertrand Du Guesclin (1320–1380) was born into a good family near Dinan. He came of age just as the Hundred Years' War began, and this accident of history established his career as a military hero. A century after his death, Brittany's beloved last duchess, Anne de Bretagne (1477–1514) captured all hearts in her short life. She married two kings of France, and endowed the province with great wealth. None the less, she was unable to secure Brittany's lasting independence, and soon after her death, the Duchy died too. In 1532, Brittany was subsumed into the rest of France.

Anon
Many thousands of Breton builders, artists and craftsmen are completely unknown. Imagine how many unsung heroes must have helped to shift the standing stones of Carnac into place, or heave those huge dolmen slabs on top of each other. We have no idea who built the churches and carved the calvaries of Finistère, or who decorated those glory-beams and pulpits with such intricate carving, but their works have lasted longer than most.

Seafarers

In 1534, Jacques Cartier (1491–1557) set sail from his native St-Malo to search for a route to China via North America. He didn't find it, but he did encounter some native Indians who told him the name of their village – Canada. And so a vast new territory was added to France's colonial possessions. The 17th and 18th centuries continued the restless scramble for trading posts across the sea, and a new profession of licensed piracy became respectable. The corsairs of St-Malo, authorised by royal charter, plundered enemy ships and became wealthy enough to build themselves the finest houses in town. Robert Surcouf (1773–1827) and René Duguay-Trouin (1673–1736) were two of the most successful. In a completely different line of entrepreneurial seafaring, Alexis Gourvennec set up Brittany Ferries in the 1970s, originally to carry cauliflowers to new markets in the UK.

Above: *Jacques Cartier, son of St-Malo*

Artists and Writers

The most celebrated artist associated with Brittany is Paul Gauguin (1848–1903), though he was no local and actually spent only a few years near Pont-Aven. Very little of his work can be seen in Brittany today. Better represented are Gauguin's associate Émile Bernard (1868–1941), Lamballe-born Mathurin Méhuet (1882–1958), and Emmanuel de la Villéon (1858–1944), from Fougères. The Romantic writer François-René de Chateaubriand (1768–1848), born in Combourg Castle and buried on St-Malo's Ile du Grand-Bé, is not much read outside France today. Better known are the science-fiction pioneer Jules Vernes (1828–1905), a native of Nantes, and Jack Kerouac (*On The Road*), born in Canada of Breton emigré parents (1922–1969).

Top: *Equestrian statue of Bernard Du Guesclin in Dinan*

Top Ten

Above: *Chapel of Notre-Dame, Port Blanc*
Right: *Detail of Guimiliau's calvary*

15

1
Carnac: Les Alignements

✚ 28C2

🚌 Reseau TIM No 01
(Plouharnel–Auray)

An extraordinary array of megaliths, many organised in mysterious lines or rows, continues to baffle and fascinate experts and visitors alike.

ℹ️ Place de l'Église
☎ 02 97 52 13 52

Musée de Préhistoire

✉️ 10 place de la Chapelle

☎ 02 97 52 22 04; www.
museedecarnac.com

🕐 Jun–Sep Mon–Fri
10–6:30 (closed Wed
am), Sat–Sun & hols
10–12, 2–6:30; Oct–
May Wed–Mon 10–12,
2–5. Closed 1–15 Jan

🍴 Cafés and restaurants
near main square and
on the seafront (€–€€);
try La Marine, place de
la Chapelle

♿ Good ✋ Moderate

La Maison de Mégaliths

✉️ Alignements du Ménec,
Route des Alignements

☎ 02 97 52 29 81

🕐 Jul–Aug daily 9–8; May–
Jun 9–7; Sep–Apr 10–5

🚌 *Petit-train* (tourist train)
from Alignements de
Ménec (€€)

♿ Good ✋ Free

It is not so much the town, a pleasant if unexceptional seaside resort, but the astonishing complexes of megaliths on its northern outskirts that attract interest in Carnac. Thousands of visitors head here to see them every year. Until 1991, the sites were freely accessible, but now the main groups of megaliths are fenced off to protect them from damage and erosion. This conservation measure, understandable if regrettable in some ways, is rather belated. For many centuries the stones have been removed, reshaped, defaced and mistakenly restored until it is impossible to know their original positions precisely, or exactly how many there were – still less what their purpose was.

A good starting point for learning more about Brittany's megaliths is the **Musée de Préhistoire** on Carnac's main square. This gives a scholarly and rather technical presentation on local antiquities and archaeological theories (ask for the English translation notes). There are three main groups of *alignements* (rows of standing stones or menhirs): Ménec, Kermario and Kerlescan, containing some 2,700 stones altogether. You can see them from the roadside, but raised viewing platforms give a clearer idea of the patterns. An information centre called **La Maison de Mégaliths** near the Alignements de Menec shows a video in French explaining the megaliths.

Other types of megalith can be found in and around Carnac, including dolmens (roofed table-like structures), tumuli (cairns) and gallery graves (*allées couvertes*). These are less mysterious in that they were all presumably used as burial places. The megalith complex at nearby Locmariaquer (► 85) can be visited on a joint ticket with Carnac's museum.

2
Côte de Granit Rose

Bizarrely shaped rocks in improbable colours make the coastline around the popular family holiday resort of Perros–Guirec one of the most memorable scenes in Brittany.

This eye-catching 20km stretch of coast takes its name from the vividly coloured rocks mainly between Perros-Guirec and Trébeurden. Dramatic rocks begin at the Ile de Bréhat, particularly noticeable at low tide when many reefs are exposed. But the small resorts of Ploumanac'h and Trégastel-Plage, further west, are the best places to see this russet rockery at its most striking, especially at sunset, when the stones take on an even fiercer glow. Not just the colours, but the weird forms they assume, are remarkable. The best way to see them is on foot. The *sentier des douaniers* (watchpath) leading around the cliffs from Perros-Guirec through the Parc Municipal to the Pointe de Ploumanac'h is one of the most enjoyable walks in Brittany (➤ 50), leading past a grand jumble of rounded boulders weathered into strange organic-looking shapes, given fanciful names like the Tortoise, the Pancakes and Napoleon's Hat.

The local rock is widely used as a building material, and when cut and polished, it sparkles beautifully and makes a most elegant finish (popular for Parisian shopfronts and luxury bathrooms). Similarly eroded rocks occur on other parts of the Breton coast, but nothing matches the rosy tints of the Pink Granite Coast.

The region around Perros-Guirec is one of Brittany's most popular tourist areas, with excellent facilities for family holidays. Inland, just to the west of Ploumanac'h, the Traouïéro valleys (Grand and Petit) offer wonderland walks along wooded creeks fringed by a chaos of huge and precariously balanced granite blocks. One valley contains an ancient tidal flour-mill, in use until the 20th century.

➕ 28C5

🍴 Plenty of cafés and restaurants in the main resorts (€–€€€)

🚌 CAT Line 15 serves the main Pink Granite Coast resorts from Lannion

🛥 Excursions to Les Sept-Iles (a puffin colony) from Perros-Guirec

ℹ Maison du Littoral, Sentier des Douaniers ☎ 02 96 91 62 77 (exhibition, guided walks) 🕐 Only open during school hols

♿ None

✋ Free

↔ Perros-Guirec (➤ 49); Trégastel (➤ 51)

Red-tinged sands near Ploumanac'h

3
Dinan

29E4

An excellent choice in the old town and by the port (€–€€€)

River trips or boat hire from the port; the Rance links with Brittany's major inland waterways

9 rue du Château
☎ 02 96 87 69 76

La Maison de la Rance

✉ Port de Dinan

☎ 02 96 87 00 40

🕐 Jul–Aug daily 10–12:30, 2–7; Apr–Jun, Sep–Nov Tue–Sun 2–6; Nov–Mar Sun 2–6

♿ Good

Inexpensive

The River Rance winds its way through the ancient town of Dinan

This picturesque medieval town of winding streets and timber-framed buildings overlooking the Rance makes a charming base for a night or two.

Standing high above the Rance estuary at what was for many centuries the lowest bridging point, Dinan was a strategic junction even in Roman times. By the 10th century it had an important Benedictine monastery, and by the 12th it was protected by high ramparts. The warrior knight of the Hundred Years' War, Bertrand Du Guesclin, was born near the town in 1320. The large, tree-lined main square is named after him and has an equestrian statue of the hero. The weekly market is held here on Thursday; at other times the square makes a useful parking area. The Fête des Remparts, a biennial medieval fair, re-creates Dinan's feudal heyday in a colourful pageant.

The Château makes a good starting point, with a museum of local history in the machicolated keep. The 18th-century Gothic-Romanesque basilica of St-Sauveur is the last resting place of Du Guesclin's heart. Dinan's other main church is St-Malo, best seen from the grounds of the Ancien Couvent des Cordeliers (a former Franciscan monastery). Many quaint buildings with sagging timbers and porticoes can be found in the old streets. Climb the Tour de l'Horloge (clock tower) for a good town view.

The steep, winding street leading down to the port is lined with picturesque, timbered merchant houses. Some now contain craft studios or shops. Terrace restaurants and cafés overlook the Rance from the quaysides. Discover all about the Rance at **La Maison de la Rance**, through models and displays inside and the flora and fauna of the marshlands reconstructed outside.

4
Fougères: Castle

The dominant feature of this shoe-making town on the Breton borderlands is a magnificent fortress, built to deter French encroachments from the east.

Built piecemeal from around AD 1166 until the 15th century, this mighty stronghold of schist and granite is one of the largest and best preserved examples of medieval fortification in France. Its various sections demonstrate the advances in warfare that took place during the Middle Ages. Unusually, it is set *below* the town rather than above it, but on what was believed to be an easily defensible site – a tight loop in the River Nançon flanked by steep cliffs. The castle consists of a series of concentric enclosures protected by massive curtain walls studded with 13 towers, and encircled by a moat of weirs and waterfalls. The structure is in excellent condition, its machicolations and loopholes intact. Despite its impregnable appearance, however, it was repeatedly attacked and captured by Du Guesclin and others, sometimes by stealth rather than force. The castle made a romantic backdrop to Balzac's novel *Les Chouans* (1829), which describes the anti-Republican uprising in vividly gory detail.

Access for today's visitors leads via a bridge over the Nançon from a picturesque old quarter of tanneries and timbered houses bright with geraniums near St-Sulpice church. The castle towers are beautifully reflected in the waters of the moat.

A walk outside the walls gives a lasting impression of the castle site, and the upper town, approached by a steep climb through public gardens, offers an excellent view of the castle's towers and ramparts near St-Léonard church.

✚ 29F4

✉ Place Pierre-Simon

☎ 02 99 99 79 59

🕐 Mid-Jun to mid-Sep 9–7; Apr–mid-Jun 9:30–12, 2–6; winter 10–12, 2–5. Closed Jan

🍴 Restaurants and cafés mainly in upper town (€–€€); try Les Voyageurs, 10 place Gambetta

🚌 Regular bus and coach services from Rennes, St-Malo, Vitré

ℹ 1 place Aristide Briand
☎ 02 99 94 12 20

♿ None

✋ Moderate

↔ Vitré (▶ 66)

Fougères' magnificent feudal castle viewed from above

5
Guimiliau: Parish Close

✚ 28B5

🍴 Ar Chupen (€), a *crêperie* near the church (43 rue du Calvaire)

♿ None

✋ Free

❓ Guided tours in July and August

One of the star examples of Finistère's enclos paroissiaux, Guimiliau's decorated calvary is a tour-de-force of 16th-century religious art.

Brittany's parish closes are unique to the region, and one of its greatest treasures. Most lie in or near the Parc Naturel Régional d'Armorique, and several of the best, including Guimiliau, are close together in the Élorn Valley near Landerneau.

The phrase *enclos paroissial* refers to the walled plot of hallowed ground around a church. Parish closes are used as graveyards, but their main interest lies in their architectural features. Typically, these consist of a triumphal gateway through which funeral processions pass, an ossuary or charnel house (used for exhumed bones) and a sculpted granite calvary depicting mostly biblical scenes. The figures are generally portrayed in contemporary Renaissance dress, so they look like something from a Shakespearean play. Today the granite carvings are weather-worn and blotched with lichen, but still remarkable for their energy and detail.

The great era of the parish close was during the 16th and 17th centuries, when communities grew rich on sea trade and linen cloth. Their wealth was used to glorify God in religious art and architecture. Villages vied with each other for the grandest and most elaborate display. Guimiliau has a vast, ornate calvary, one of the largest in the area, with over 200 separate figures over an arched base, including the Virgin, St Peter, St John and St Yves with Christ. Look out, too, for a horrific scene showing a young girl being torn apart by demons. This is Catell Gollet, whose downfall occurred when she stole consecrated wafers for her handsome lover (the Devil in disguise). The church interior is crammed with decoration, including wonderful woodwork and altarpieces, and a finely carved pulpit and 17th-century organ.

Guimiliau's exquisite calvary includes over 200 figures

Opposite: The exhibition hall at Brest's outstanding sea centre

6
Océanopolis, Brest

Brest's ambitious aquarium explores many aspects of the sea and the life within it, both off the Breton coast and worldwide.

This huge futuristic complex down by the docks is a major regional attraction in any terms. You could easily spend the best part of a day exploring all its 1,000-plus species and many exhibits relating to the seas and marine life of Brittany and other parts of the world. Expansion has resulted in a tripartite exhibition zone of pavilions linked by covered walkways. It has 42 separate aquariums, some containing up to a million litres of water.

The Temperate Pavilion concentrates on the Breton coastal waters and the Finistère fishing industry. Its huge tanks hold a massive number of local marine species, with special emphasis on those of economic importance (seaweeds, edible fish etc). There's also a seal tank, an oceanography exhibition and a jellyfish collection. The Tropical Pavilion has a shark tank and a colourful array of coral-reef fish, all in beautifully realistic settings. A diver feeds the fish, and a tropical greenhouse simulates a mangrove swamp. The Polar Pavilion has a tank of endearingly comical penguins (strategically placed windows show how they chug through the water). Other species from chillier climes seem happily housed in convincingly authentic pack ice. Special events and temporary exhibitions take place and there are multimedia presentations.

The aim is to educate as well as amuse. Some visitors detect with regret a recent trend towards mere entertainment. For all that, it's a worthwhile place, easily the best of its kind in Brittany despite much competition and steep entrance charges.

www.oceanopolis.com

🞦 28A4

✉ Port de Plaisance du Moulin-Blanc, 2km east of city centre

☎ 02 98 34 40 40

🌐 Apr–Sep daily 9–6; winter 10–5 (closed Mon except school hols). Last tickets sold one hour before closing time

🍴 Several on-site eating places: restaurant, self-service café, terrace, takeaway (€–€€) – no entrance charge

🚌 No 7 from city centre

⛴ Le Fret ferry; harbour trips

✈ Brest-Guipavas Airport; domestic and international flights

ℹ 8 Avenue Clémenceau; ☎ 02 98 44 24 96

♿ Very good

✋ Expensive

⬌ Central Brest (➤ 31–32)

7
Presqu'île de Crozon

🍴 Restaurants at Le Fret, Camaret and Morgat (€€)

🚌 Lines 43 and 10 serve the peninsula's main centres

⛴ Boat trips/ferry services from Le Fret, Camaret and Morgat

ℹ Main office in the old railway station, Crozon (☎ 02 98 26 17 18); Camaret (☎ 02 98 27 93 60); and seasonal office at Morgat (☎ 02 98 27 29 49)

♿ None

Below: *This natural arch forms a bridge over the sea at Pointe de Dinan*

Opposite: *Wide beaches and high cliffs viewed from Pointe de Penhir*

Interesting museums and small, low-key resorts with good fish restaurants add to the natural attractions of one of Finistère's most exhilarating coastal headlands.

This hammerhead peninsula lunges towards the Atlantic in a lather of wave-lashed fury, the foaming tongue of Finistère's mad-dog profile. It forms part of the Parc Naturel Régional d'Armorique, and has some spectacular scenery, particularly at its westerly extremities. It has little intensive farming and virtually no heavy industry. A circular tour makes an exciting day-trip, with time for breezy cliff walks or a picnic, or visits to some of its little *ecomusées*. The pleasingly understated fishing village resorts nestling in the indented coast may tempt you for a longer stay.

The old town of Le Faou, with its charmingly restored 17th-century houses and church, makes a good starting point (its attractive food shops stock picnic provisions). Detour though the wooded estuary scenery around Térénez to the evocative, romantically set ruins of the **Abbaye de Landévennec** at the mouth of the Aulne. This Romanesque monastery was founded in the 5th century by St Guénolé. A small museum on monastic history can be visited in a neighbouring convent building, while a Benedictine community occupies modern premises near by.

The cider museum and parish close at Argol, and the **Musée de l'École Rurale** at Trégarvan (a typical village schoolroom of the early 20th century), are worth a visit too.

Continuing along the coastal route takes you past Le Fret, a pretty port with marvellous views of the Rade de Brest, and a ferry service to Brest. The Pointe des Espagnols to the north is an even more spectacular viewpoint. To the east lies Ile Longue, a nuclear submarine base (understandably, a no-go area for tourists).

Crozon, the village that gives its name to the peninsula, is of no great interest, but the jagged headlands beyond (Pointe des Espagnols, Pointe de Pen-Hir and Pointe de Dinan) vie with each other for coastal charisma. The road to Pen-Hir passes the Alignements de Lagatjar (a group of standing stones), and a little museum in a wartime blockhouse commemorating the merchant seamen who died in convoy attacks during the Battle of the Atlantic. The rocky islets sprinkled off the coast at Pointe de Pen-Hir are called the Tas de Pois (Heap of Peas). Camaret-sur-Mer is a little lobster port sheltered by a natural shingle bank called the Sillon. On this stand a charming miniature Vauban fortress containing a small exhibition, and a clutch of good fish restaurants. The tiny pilgrim chapel of Notre-Dame-de-Rocamadour, with model votive ships hanging above the nave, demonstrates the powerful influence of the sea on the local community. In September, a Blessing of the Sea ceremony is held. Though fishing has declined here, Camaret is something of an artists' enclave; several attractive craft studios are scattered around the village.

Morgat, a former tuna-fishing port, is another attractive sheltered resort, these days a yachting haven with a good sandy beach backed by pine trees. Boat excursions visit a group of caves with vivid mineral colourations. Cap de la Chèvre, to the south, is another scenic rocky headland, with breezy cliff walks. The placid route along the southern coast reveals several gorgeous sandy beaches.

Musée de l'Ancienne Abbaye de Landévennec

 Abbaye de Landévennec

 02 98 27 35 90

 Jul–Aug daily 10–7; May–Jun Sun–Fri 2–6; Sep daily 10–6; Oct–Apr Sun 2–6

 Moderate

 Few

Musée de l'École Rurale

 Trégarvan

02 98 26 04 72

Jul–Aug daily 10:30–7; 2–5 only off-peak. Closed Sat & Sun Dec–Feb

 Moderate Few

8
Quimper

Musée Départemental Breton

✉ 1 rue du Roi Gradlon

☎ 02 98 95 21 60

🕐 Jun–Sep daily 9–6; Oct–May 9–12, 2–5 (closed Sun AM, Mon & hols)

♿ Good

✋ Moderate

Musée des Beaux-Arts

✉ 40 place St-Corentin

☎ 02 98 95 45 20

🕐 Jul–Aug daily 10–7; Jun & Sep daily 10–12, 2–6; reduced hours off-peak (closed Tue & Sun AM)

♿ Good

✋ Moderate

Quimper's cobbled old quarter

Cornouaille's capital is one of Brittany's most charming historic cities, a pleasure for shopping and strolling, especially if you like the region's cheerful, hand-decorated ceramics.

Good road and rail links, even an international airport, make Quimper easily accessible by public transport. A day-trip gives ample time to enjoy its quintessentially Breton atmosphere, especially on market day. It's a lively, bustling place with plenty of cultural activity, most noticeable during its weeklong summer Festival de Cornouaille, when Breton costume is *de rigueur*, and Celtic folk groups converge from far and wide.

The Breton name for the town derives from the word *kemper*, meeting place of rivers. The Steir and Odet run throughout the old quarter lined with pavement cafés and brasseries in Parisian style. Quimper is a good place for gourmet food shopping and dining. On the south bank of the Odet (where you'll find the tourist office) rises Mount Frugy, a wooded hill with panoramic picnic potential.

Crossing the river into the old town, the twin-spired Cathédrale St-Corentin (under restoration) makes an immediate impact. It dates from the 13th–15th centuries, though its towers are more recent. Near by the **Musée**

Départemental Breton displays an extensive collection of pottery, costumes and furniture. The **Musée des Beaux-Arts**, in the town hall, contains an assortment of Pont-Aven School art. The old quarter stretches mainly west of the cathedral, past many quaint flower-decked, dormered houses and *hotels particuliers* (mansions).

Quimper dates from Roman times, when a settlement called *Aquilonia* grew up on the site of present-day Locmaria, where Quimper's ceramics industry developed, producing handpainted *paysan* designs of blue and yellow flowers or birds. Oldest of its factories is the Faïenceries HB-Henriot (☎ 02 98 90 09 36; tours Mar–Oct). The Musée de la Faïence (www.quimper.faiences.com) has a superb display of Quimper ware.

9
St-Malo

The most appealing of any of the Channel ports, the walled citadel of St–Malo deserves more than a cursory glance en route to the ferry terminal, and there's plenty to see near by.

 29E5

🍴 Good restaurants, cafés and bars throughout the old town (€–€€€)

St-Malo is many visitors' first experience of Brittany. Its attractive setting and architecture, excellent hotels and restaurants, sandy beaches and lively ambience make this no bad landfall. It is named after a Welsh monk, St Maclow, who founded a religious community in Aleth (now St-Servan, a suburb of St-Malo). St-Malo developed a strong seafaring tradition and prospered greatly from trade with Spain and the Americas. For a time it was an independent republic. During World War II, much of the old town was completely destroyed, but later painstakingly reconstructed in its original 18th-century style.

The walled city (*intra muros*) is the most interesting part. Park outside the walls and explore on foot. A rampart walk gives a splendid overview of the port's setting. On the seaward side lie sandy beaches and tidal islets. The main points of interest are the Cathédrale St-Vincent with bright modern glass, and the Château de la Duchesse Anne near the Porte St-Vincent, which contains the **Musée de la Ville** (town museum).

West of the walled town, the St-Servan district is worth a visit for marvellous views of the port and marina from the Aleth headland. The Tour Solidor contains a small museum dedicated to Cape Horn sailors. East of St-Malo are the resorts of Paramé and Rothéneuf, with good beaches. In Rothéneuf visit the Manoir Limoëlou, former home of Jacques Cartier, discoverer of Canada, and Les Rochers Sculptés, a collection of grotesque figures carved from the natural clifftop rocks by a local priest.

St-Malo's new aquarium, on the route to Rennes is no match for Brest's Océanopolis (➤ 21).

🚌 Regular services to Rennes, Mont-St-Michel, Dinard and the Emerald Coast

🚉 SNCF routes to Rennes and Normandy

🚢 Brittany Ferries (Portsmouth, UK); Rance river trips to Dinan; regular services to Channel Isles

✈️ Dinard–St-Malo airport; Aurigny & Ryanair services to UK/Channel Isles

ℹ️ Esplanade St-Vincent ☎ 02 99 56 64 48

↔️ Dinard (➤ 57), Cancale (➤ 56)

Musée de la Ville

☎ 02 99 40 71 57

🕐 Apr–Sep daily 10–12, 2–6. Closed Mon in winter

♿ None 👁 Moderate

Old St-Malo was built on what used to be an island

10
St-Pierre Cathedral, Nantes

✚ 77D3

✉ Place St-Pierre

🕐 Daily, apart from during Mass. Renovations are in progress and parts of the cathedral could be closed to visitors

🍴 Plenty of eating places near the castle (€–€€€)

♿ Few ✋ Free

↔ Nantes (➤ 76–78)

Soaring vaults of bright stone give a lasting sense of space and light inside this impressive cathedral in the upper town.

Undaunted by its proximity to the formidable Château des Ducs de Bretagne (➤ 76), Nantes' cathedral is built of clear, white tufa – quite a contrast to the sombre, weather-worn granite found in most Breton churches. Building works on St-Pierre began in 1434, on the site of an earlier Romanesque building, but it wasn't completed for another four and a half centuries. The towers were added in 1508. For all that, it seems a surprisingly coherent piece of Gothic workmanship, and post-war restoration work has given it a spruce and cared-for look. Its history, however, has been anything but tranquil. In 1800 a massive ammunition explosion in the nearby castle shattered all its precious 15th-century stained glass. During the Revolution, it served as a barn, it was bombed during World War II, and damaged by a fire in 1971, after which its interior had to be completely cleaned yet again. Today, it is light, airy and spacious.

Nantes' dazzling white tufa cathedral dominates the upper town

The replacement windows in the choir (containing over 500sq m of modern stained glass) took over 12 years to create, and these alone justify a visit. St-Pierre's other main highlight is the magnificent Renaissance tomb of François II, the last Duke of Brittany, sculpted by the master-craftsman Michel Colombe between 1502 and 1507. The two main effigies depict François and his wife Margaret (parents of the Duchess Anne), and the corner statues are personifications of Justice, Fortitude, Temperance and Prudence. This elaborate tomb was commissioned by Anne in memory of her parents, and she asked that her heart be placed in it after her own death. Her wish was granted, though the heart vanished at some point during the Revolution. Another noteworthy 19th-century tomb commemorates General Lamoricière, famed for his adventures in Algeria.

What to See

Above: *Half-timbering in Rennes*
Right: *Wild boar statue outside Château de Rosanbo*

27

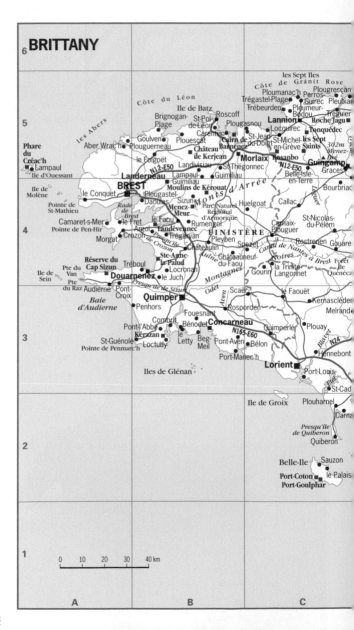

BRITTANY

les Sept Iles
Côte de Gránit Rose
Ploumanac'h · Perros- · Plougrescant
Trégastel-Plage · Guirec · Pleubian
Trébeurden · Pleumeur- · Pleubian
· Bodou · Tréguier

Côte du Léon
Brignogan- · Ile de Batz · Roscoff
Plage · St-Pol- · Plougasnou
Goulven · de-Léon · Lannion · Roche Jagu
Aber Wrac'h · Plouguerneau · Carentec · St-Jean · Tonquédec
Phare · le Folgoët · Plouescat · Château · du-Doigt · les Sept
du · Landivisiau · de Kerjean · St-Michel- · Saints · Guingamp
Créac'h · en-Grève · Menez- · N12-E50
Lampaul · Lampaul · St-Thégonnec · Belle-Isle- · Graces
Ile d'Ouessant · Guimiliau · en-Terre

Ile de · Landerneau · Guimiliau · Bourbriac
Molène · BREST · Plougastel- · Moulins de Kérouat
· Daoulas · Menez- · d'Arrée · Callac
Pointe de · le Conquet · Meur · Parc Naturel · Huelgoat
St-Mathieu · Rade · le Faou · Régional
· de · Landévennec · d'Armorique · St-Nicolas-
Camaret-s-Mer · Brest · Argol · Rumengol · Carhaix- · du-Pélem
Pointe de Pen-Hir · le Fret · Trégarvan · Pleyben · Plouguer · Rostrenen · Gouare
Morgat · Crozon · Châteaulin · Spezet · FINISTÈRE · Forêt
· Presqu'île · Châteauneuf- · Canal de Nantes à Brest · de
Réserve du · de Crozon · Ste-Anne- · du-Faou · Gourin · la Trinité · Quénéca
Cap Sizun · la-Palud · Locronan · Montagnes · Langonnet
Ile de · Pte du · Tréboul · le Juch · Oder · Scaër · le Faouët
Sein · Van · Douarnenez · Aulne · Kernascléden
· Pte · Audierne · Pont- · Quimper · Aven · Rosporden · Melrand
du Raz · Croix · Penhors · Fouesnant · Quimperlé · Plouay
Baie · Combrit · Bénodet · Concarneau · N165-E60 · N24
d'Audierne · Pont-l'Abbé · Letty · Beg- · Pont-Aven · Bélon · Hennebont
St-Guénolé · Kérazan · Meil · Port-Manec'h · Lorient · Port-Louis
Pointe de Penmarc'h · Loctudy · · St-Cad
Iles de Glénan · Ile de Groix · Plouharnel · Carna

Presqu'île
de Quiberon · Quiberon

Belle-Ile · Sauzon
Port-Coton · le Palais
Port-Goulphar

0 10 20 30   40 km

A   B   C

Finistère

Finistère is the most Breton part of Brittany, a land of priests and pagans, pierced steeples and spectacular parish closes, where fervent piety mingles with ancient superstition. Here, more than anywhere, you may find traditional customs and costumes, and hear Breton spoken. The fertile Ceinture d'Or (Golden Belt) stretches along the north coast, producing early vegetables, but Brittany's age-old maritime economy still figures large in the fishing ports of Douarnenez, Concarneau and Roscoff.

The dramatic extremities of Crozon and Sizun make memorable touring, and the islands of Ouessant and Batz have their own quiet charm. Inland, the wild uplands of the Monts d'Arrée and Montagnes Noires are a chance to escape coastal crowds; a few remnants of Brittany's ancient forests survive at Huelgoat. In the south, the lush wooded estuaries of the Odet and the Aven create the idyllic watercolours immortalised by Pont-Aven's 19th-century artists.

> *' Two enemies, earth and sea, man and nature, meet in eternal conflict. '*
>
> JULES MICHELET
> *Histoire de France,*
> published in 23 volumes
> 1833–1878

What to See in Finistère

BÉNODET ✪✪

In the Middle Ages, Bénodet's income sprang from trading salt, fish and wine. Today its economic mainstay is tourism. Apart from its lighthouses and a scrap of fortress, the town has few notable sights or historic buildings. Its popularity is based on the attractions of its natural setting at the mouth of the wooded Odet estuary, and a series of excellent beaches. Families converge to take advantage of Bénodet's resort amenities in summer, which include sailing in Le Letty's tidal lagoon. Opened in 2003, the **Musée du Bord de Mer** explains the history of yachting and sailing at Bénodet. For more seclusion, take the graceful modern bridge or shuttle ferry across the river to Ste-Marine, a charming collection of cottages amid pine trees. Boat trips up the River Odet, or to the Iles de Glénan in the Baie de Concarneau, are highly recommended.

BREST ✪✪

Brest's strategic location on a magnificent natural harbour (Rade de Brest) at the edge of western Europe has been its fortune, and its undoing. The Romans first spotted its potential and built a camp in the 3rd century. The settlement was fortified by the counts of Léon in the 12th century, and occupied by the English for part of the Hundred Years' War. Louis XIII chose it as his principal naval base in the 17th century. Brest expanded and prospered during the seafaring centuries that followed,

Sidebar

✚ 28B3
🍴 Good choice throughout resort (€–€€€)
🚌 No 16 (Quimper)
🚢 Trips on the Odet and to Iles de Glénan
ℹ 29 avenue de la Mer
☎ 02 98 57 00 14

Musée du Bord de Mer
✉ 29 avenue de la Mer
☎ 02 98 57 00 14
🕐 Jun–Sep daily 10–7
♿ Good 🏷 Moderate

Yachts moored at the charming seaside resort of Bénodet

✚ 28A4
🍴 Good choice around main sights (€–€€€)
🚌 Major route-hub for public transport; many inner-city buses
🚢 Ferry to Le Fret; harbour cruises
ℹ 8 Avenue Clémenceau
☎ 02 98 44 24 96

The Madeleine Tower of Brest's castle houses the Musée de la Marine

though its harbour was maintained for defensive rather than trade purposes, and it never accrued the wealth of other Breton seaports. During German Occupation, Brest became a U-Boat base, plaguing transatlantic convoys and becoming the unwilling target of sustained Allied bombardment towards the end of the war. When Brest fell in 1944, it was utterly devastated. Vast post-war investment has rebuilt, if not entirely revitalised the town in a functional modern style of concrete high-rises. It retains none of its former charm, but is worth a visit for its streamlined docks and roadstead views, and several interesting sights. A university town, it has plenty of cultural activities and events. Harbour cruises are highly recommended.

The Castle and the neighbouring Cours Dajot promenade give excellent views of the Rade de Brest. Built between the 12th and 17th centuries, it miraculously withstood the bombs of World War II and now houses both the naval headquarters and the **Musée de la Marine** (Maritime Museum). Its eclectic displays include splendid cedar figure-heads, a manned torpedo vessel from World War II and a Vietnamese refugee boat. Near the castle stands the massive Pont de Recouvrance, an impressive piece of engineering and Europe's highest swing-bridge, and the 15th-century Tour Tanguy, containing a museum of Old Brest, which gives an enlightening view of how the port once looked. In the city centre, the **Musée des Beaux-Arts** (Fine Arts Museum) contains a collection of Pont-Aven paintings (closed Tue). The church of St-Louis is an interesting example of post-war architecture with bright windows of jagged modern glass.

On the north side of town, not far from the Océanopolis aquarium (► 21), at Port de Plaisance du Moulin-Blanc, the **Conservatoire Botanique National**, dedicated to the preservation of rare and endangered species, will delight plant-lovers.

Musée de la Marine
- ✉ Château de Brest
- ☎ 02 98 22 12 39
- 🕐 Apr–mid-Sep daily 10–6:30; mid-Sep to mid-Mar 10–noon, 2–6. Closed Tue mid-Dec–Jan & hols
- ♿ None 💰 Moderate

Musée des Beaux-Arts
- ✉ 24 rue Traverse
- ☎ 02 98 00 87 96
- 🕐 Daily 10–12, 2–6. Closed Tue, Sun AM & hols
- ♿ None 💰 Moderate

Conservatoire Botanique National
- ✉ 52 allée du Bot
- ☎ 02 98 02 46 00
- 🕐 Garden daily 9–6 (until 8 in summer); Pavillon d'Acceuil Wed & Sun 2–4:30; greenhouses Jul–mid-Sep Sun–Thu 2–5:30
- ♿ Few
- 💰 Free to garden; moderate to visitor centre & greenhouses

CAP SIZUN ✪✪✪

Sizun's jagged finger stretches far into the Atlantic, ending in a dramatic climax at the Pointe du Raz, where a statue of Notre-Dame-des-Naufragés (Our Lady of the Shipwrecked) is aptly placed. Out to sea, the Ile de Sein barely rises above the waterline, a treacherous obstacle to shipping. Wear sensible shoes if you want to walk around the headland as the rocks can be very slippery, and take binoculars if you are keen on birdwatching. The **Réserve de Goulien** is a popular destination during the nesting season. Audierne has another large nature reserve. The **Maison de la Baie** organises nature walks.

Sizun is full of legends: Tristan and Isolde and the lost city of Ys among them. Some say the souls of the drowned rise up at the Baie des Trépassés on All-Hallows Day, and certainly a body washes up from time to time. Apart from the fishing ports of Douarnenez and Audierne, there are no large settlements. Inland, the scenery consists of quiet, uneventful farmland. Pont-Croix is worth a look for its unusual gabled church (Notre-Dame-du-Roscudon). Audierne has a fine setting on the Goyen estuary, large fish farms (visitors welcome), and the impressive **Planète Aquarium** containing a comprehensive collection of Breton marine species.

✚ 28A4

Réserve de Goulien

✉ Cap Sizun
☎ 02 98 70 13 53
🕑 Apr–Aug. Guided tours Jul–Aug daily; Apr–Jun Sat & Sun
♿ None
👣 Moderate

Maison de la Baie

✉ St-Vio, Trégeunnec
☎ 02 98 82 37 99
🕑 Jul–Oct; call for programme of events
♿ None
👣 Moderate

Planète Aquarium

✉ Rue du Goyen, Audierne
☎ 02 98 70 03 03
🕑 May–Sep daily 10–7; Jul–Aug 10–10; Oct–Apr school hols only 2–5
♿ Good 👣 Expensive

CHÂTEAU DE KERJEAN ✪✪

The Château de Kerjean is one of Brittany's finest Renaissance manors. Set in 20 hectares of sweeping parkland, the château's gabled roofline rises above high ramparts, beyond a drawbridge and a deep moat. It dates from the late 16th century, and suffered much damage during the Revolution, when its last *aristo* was guillotined. In 1911 it passed into State hands. Since then it has been restored and converted into a cultural centre and museum of traditional Breton furniture. As well as a film show, learn about Château life in the 18th century through workshops.

www.chateau-de-kerjean.com
✚ 28B5
✉ St-Vougay
☎ 02 98 69 93 69
🕑 Jul–Aug daily 10–7 (closed Tue); Nov–Mar Wed & Sun 2–5
♿ None
👣 Moderate

Pointe du Raz, Cap Sizun

33

A Drive around Cap Sizun

Distance
80km – some walking

Time
Allow about half a day –
longer with extensive walks or
picnics

Start/end point
Douarnenez
 28B4

Lunch
Hotel de la Baie des
Trépassés (€€) (► 93)

A drive round some of Finistère's most exciting headlands.

From Douarnenez, take the north coast road (D7), ducking northwards at Pointe du Millier.

A few minutes walk to the point offers a splendid view of the bay. Further west, Pointe de Beuzec (accessible by car) has similar views.

Return to the D7 and head westwards to the Reserve de Goulien at Cap Sizun.

This famous bird sanctuary on a wild granite cape is best visited between April and mid-July when a host of seabirds rear their young on the dark rocky cliffs of Castel-ar-Roc'h.

Seabirds frequent the craggy rocks at Pointe du Raz

Return to the D7 again and continue 6km westwards to the Pointe de Brézellec (north off the road).

Park near the lighthouse and enjoy a magnificent vantage point of serrated rocks and cliffs.

Continue west to the Pointe du Van.

A lengthy walk leads to a desolate treeless headland of stone and moss, less spectacular than Pointe du Raz, but less crowded. The cliffs here are dangerous. One lonely hotel guards the headland.

Follow the coast road south past the Baie des Trépassés.

This sweeping crescent of firm sand may look inviting, but the currents are strong. In a gale, it's a terrifying sight.

Join the D784 and head west for 2.5km to the Pointe du Raz, the highlight of the journey

Technically this is not France's most westerly point. The point snakes out to sea, ending in razor pinnacles. A path leads round the rocky point with safety ropes, but take care; the rocks are slippery and freak waves may sweep you off.

Return to Douarnenez along the D784 via Audierne, then the D765 via Pont–Croix.

Opposite: Pleasure boats and commercial vessels share the calm waters around Concarneau

CONCARNEAU ✪✪

Fishing is on the decline in Concarneau (once one of France's most important ports), but it still has a sizeable fleet and lands varied catches in the modern, shed-like fish market by the Arrière-Port. If you arrive early enough, you can see the *criée* (fish auction) in full swing. An enterprising organisation called **A l'Assault des Remparts** offers guided tours (some in English) of the old town, including visits to the harbour, a working trawler and the quayside fish auction. The evening tours are particularly interesting, when you can see the boats arrive to unload their catches sometime after midnight.

Concarneau's most charming district is the medieval old town, or Ville Close on a rocky island protected by granite ramparts and a fortified bridge. It played a key role during the Hundred Years' War. Vauban strengthened it during the 17th century. Today tourists crowd unhindered over the drawbridge to explore quaint old streets and attractive souvenir shops. The Ville Close's best sight is the **Musée de la Pêche**, a well-displayed exhibition on the fishing industry with ancient sardine tins and giant scooping nets. An old trawler moored by the walls reveals the cramped and spartan conditions of life at sea. You can climb the ramparts for good views of the port.

Beaches stretch either side of the town, but they are not Brittany's best. Boat trips from Concarneau visit the Îles de Glénan and the Odet estuary. In late August, Concarneau's Fête des Filets Bleus (Blue Nets Festival) attracts many visitors.

➕ 28B3

🍴 Snacks and fast food within the Ville Close; the best restaurants are around the port in the main part of town (€–€€)

🚌 No 14 (Quimper–Pont-Aven–Moëlan-sur-Mer); No 20 to Rosporden

🚢 Odet, Îles de Glénan and bay cruises

ℹ Quai d'Aiguillon
　☎ 02 98 97 01 44

A l'Assault des Remparts

☎ 02 98 50 5518
🎟 Moderate
❓ Escorted or multilingual audio-guides

Musée de la Pêche

✉ 3 rue Vauban, Ville-Close
☎ 02 98 97 10 20
🕐 Jul–Aug daily 9:30–8; off-peak 10–12, 2–6
♿ Good (main museum only, not the trawler)
🎟 Expensive

GUIMILIAU (➤ 20, TOP TEN)

ILE D'OUESSANT

Ouessant is the largest of eight islands scattered off the west coast of Finistère, a treacherous obstacle course for one of the world's busiest shipping lanes. Despite all the lighthouses and warning beacons that guard the reefs, disasters still occur, notably the *Amoco Cadiz*, which foundered in 1978, and the *Erika* in 1999. The currents here are among the swiftest in Europe and the islands are often shrouded in fog.

Ouessant (anglicised as Ushant) is one of Finistère's remotest communities, yet it is easily reached on a fast ferry from Le Conquet or Brest. In fine weather (preferably calm!) a day-trip is highly recommendable. Ouessant's traditional matriarchal way of life has all but vanished on the mainland, and although the island now relies increasingly on tourism for its revenue, the older social patterns still persist. It is also an important marine conservation area, and forms part of the Parc Naturel Régional d'Armorique. Ouessant's maritime climate is surprisingly mild in winter. Seaweed processing is a local industry.

Ferry passengers alight at the Baie du Stiff where two lighthouses (ancient and modern) guard the eastern headlands. From here the best way to explore the island is by bike (for hire at the port or the main village of Lampaul). Ouessant (7km by 4km) is rather too large to see on foot in a single day and simple accommodation and restaurants can be found in Lampaul. The churchyard here contains a monument to the many islanders lost at sea. The main sights on the island are the **Ecomusée de Niou**, housed in two tiny cottages displaying a typical seafaring home of the 19th century, and numerous costumes, tools and other exhibits. On the west coast, the Phare du Creac'h contains a lighthouse museum, the **Musée des Phares et Balises**, highlighting the elaborate coastal warning system of western Brittany. The remaining pleasures of Ouessant lie mostly out of doors, in its dramatic coastal scenery, wildlife and open heathland where sheep roam freely. Many of the white cottages have blue doors and shutters, the colour of the protecting Virgin's robes.

✚ 28A5

🍴 Several simple eating places in and around Lampaul (€–€€)

ℹ Place de l'Englise, Oussant
☎ 02 98 48 85 83

Ecomusée de Niou

✉ Niou Uhella
☎ 02 98 48 86 37
🕐 Apr–Sep 10:30–6:30; Oct, Feb–Mar 10–5:30; Nov–Jan 1:30–5
♿ None
✋ Moderate (joint ticket)

Musée des Phares et Balises

✉ Phare du Créac'h
☎ 02 98 48 80 70
🕐 Apr–Sep 10:30–6:30; Oct, Feb–Mar 10–5:30; Nov–Jan 1:30–5. Night visits Jul–Aug 9–11PM
♿ None
✋ Moderate (joint ticket)

DID YOU KNOW?

The perils Finistère's low-lying offshore islands present to shipping are emphasised in an old rhyme: '*Qui voit Molène, voit sa peine; Qui voit Ouessant, voit son sang; Qui voit Sein, voit sa fin!*' Roughly translated, this means: 'If you see Molène, you've got problems; If you see Ouessant, you're in bad trouble; If you see Sein, you've had it!'

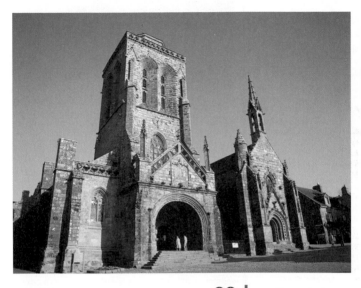

LOCRONAN ✪✪

Even when besieged by summer visitors, Locronan's charms are undeniable. Its perfect Renaissance square of gold-grey buildings is as pretty as a film-set, which, indeed, it has been from time to time. Many of the former merchants' houses have been converted into smart shops, restaurants and hotels. A browse through its craft studios is an ideal way of choosing some Breton souvenirs. Locronan's wealth originated from the manufacture of sailcloth, and for a glorious period during the 17th century it single-handedly supplied much of Europe's maritime rigging. When Louis XIV abolished its privileged monopoly, Locronan's economy collapsed. The church of St-Ronan is one of the most striking monuments, in 15th-century Ogival Flamboyant style. Stained glass marks scenes of the Passion, while the carved pulpit recounts its patron saint's life. St Ronan was an Irish missionary, and his penitential climb each day up the hill behind the town is re-enacted by annual processions called *Troménies*.

A short distance from Locronan, the seaside chapel of Ste-Anne-la-Palud is the scene of another pious ritual, one of the finest *pardon* ceremonies in Brittany (late August) with torchlit processions and Breton costumes. The object of veneration is a painted granite statue of St Anne dating from 1548.

✚ 28B4

🍴 Plenty of choice in and around the church square, such as Ty Coz (€) place de l'Eglise, or the Hotel du Prieuré, rue du Prieuré (€€)

🚌 No 10 (Quimper–Plomodiern route)

ℹ️ Place de la Mairie
☎ 02 98 91 70 14

Locronan's 15th-century church is dedicated to the Irish missionary St Ronan

Charming half-timbered buildings in Morlaix

🔲 28B5

🍴 Good choice in the old
   town (€–€€)

🚌 Many routes converge
   from Lannion, Roscoff,
   Carhaix-Plouguer etc

🚆 SNCF connections to
   Roscoff, Lannion, Brest
   and St-Brieuc

ℹ️ Place des Otages

☎ 02 98 62 14 94

Coreff Brewery

✉️ 1 place de la Madeleine

☎ 02 98 63 41 92

🕐 Guided tours Jul–Aug
   Mon–Fri 11 & 2

♿ Few

🎟️ Free

Maison de la Reine Anne

✉️ 9 rue du Mur

☎ 02 98 88 23 26

🕐 Jul–Aug 10–6:30; off-
   peak 10–12, 2:30–5:30.
   Closed Mon

♿ None

🎟️ Cheap

Musée de Morlaix

✉️ Place des Jacobins

☎ 02 98 88 68 88

🕐 Jul–Aug daily 11–6:30;
   Oct–Mar & Jun Wed–Sat
   1:30–6; Apr–May & Sep
   Wed–Sun 1:30–6

♿ Good

🎟️ Moderate

MORLAIX ✪✪

The town's location at the head of a dramatic estuary gave it a leading role in the maritime trade of the Renaissance, and from embryonic origins as a Gaullish defence camp it burgeoned into a thriving port prospering on fishing, linen, shipbuilding, tobacco-smuggling – and piracy. Like St-Malo, Morlaix was a corsair town, and its daring raids on foreign shipping provoked reprisals. After the English sacked the town in 1522, Morlaix adopted a truculent motto (a pun on its name): 'S'ils te mordent, mords-les' ('If they bite you, bite them back!'), and constructed the Château du Taureau to guard the bay. Today Morlaix is a delightful place, full of salty atmosphere and easy to explore. The old town lies close to the feet of a giant granite viaduct astride the estuarial valley. Northwards stretch the wharves of the canalised port, jostling with clanking pleasure craft and cargo boats. Overlooking it is the former 18th-century Seita tobacco factory. Also of interest is the **Coreff Brewery**, originally set up in 1985 by a couple of real ale enthusiasts. Coreff beer is a prized product, and not widely available. Visitors get a free tasting. Beyond the viaduct (which you can walk across for excellent views), quaint steep alleys called *venelles* trickle through a maze of churches and charming timbered buildings, some in an elaborate local style called 'lantern houses'. The **Maison de la Reine Anne** is the best of these (see the skylit interior). The **Musée de Morlaix** is well worth a look for its art collection, which is temporarily housed in Les Jacobin. Eventually the museum will be installed at a new site.

MONTS D'ARRÉE ⬤⬤

Aeons ago, these ancient granite hills were once as high as the Alps. Now the elements have eroded them to rounded stumps covered with gorse moors. Despite their modest height, the summits make awesome vantage points. The lonelier, less accessible stretches provide important wildlife sanctuaries. Until the last century, wolves roamed wild and dangerously hungry in winter. Today there are no more wolves, but you may encounter deer, otters and wild boar. Much of the Monts d'Arrée massif forms part of the Parc Naturel Régional d'Armorique, a diverse conservation zone encompassing hills and woodland, the tranquil Aulne estuary, the coast of Crozon and the Ouessant archipelago. A dozen or so well-presented little museums sprinkled throughout the park show various aspects of traditional rural life. The park's main information centre is at Menez-Meur, a wooded estate with a zoo park, and holds temporary exhibitions on Breton life. Huelgoat is the main community of a last vestige of Brittany's *argoat* or inland forest. Devastated by the hurricane of October 1987, there are few venerable trees left, but giant mossy boulders, fern-filled grottoes and a placid lake add interest to local walks.

✚ 28B4

🍴 Few and far between. Most options are in Huelgoat (€–€€)

🚌 Nos 52 and 61 serve Huelgoat but no scheduled routes traverse the wilder zones

ℹ️ Menez-Meur
☎ 02 98 68 81 71

PONT-AVEN ⬤⬤

Few of the watermills that once filled the town of Pont-Aven remain, but its picturesque riverside houses would still be recognisable to the painters who flocked here during the 19th century. The most notable member of the Pont-Aven School was Gauguin, though few of his works are on display at the Musée de Pont-Aven's art collection.

A wander through the old streets and nearby woods, however, will evoke many of the scenes he painted, notably the charming Chapelle de Trémalo, where a sallow crucifix in the nave was the inspiration for his startling *Christ Jaune*. Pont-Aven's popularity with visitors continues unabated, its natural attractions now supplemented by good restaurants, hotels and shops. Downstream, the Aven estuary passes through strikingly beautiful scenery.

✚ 28B3

🍴 Good if pricey choices in town (€€–€€€)

🚌 Nos 14, 21 (Riec–Concarneau–Quimper)

🚢 Estuary cruises to Port-Manec'h

ℹ️ 5 place de l'Hôtel de Ville
☎ 02 98 06 04 70

Musée de Pont-Aven

✉️ Place de l'Hôtel de Ville
☎ 02 98 06 14 43
🕐 Jul–Aug daily 10–7; Sep–Jun 10–12:30, 2–6. Closed Jan
♿ Good
🎫 Moderate

One of Gauguin's paintings in the Pont-Aven Museum

Drive in the Monts d'Arrée

Distance
60km

Time
Allow a day if you want to see most of the sights, and have a walk.

Start/end point
Sizun
 28B4

Lunch
Restaurants are scarce, and most museums do not have coffee shops. Take a picnic with you

Sizun makes a pleasant starting point.

Its church has elaborate panelled vaulting and decorated beams, and a parish close with a magnificent triumphal arch. The Maison de la Rivière and the Maison du Lac deal with aspects of the local waterways and their wildlife.

From Sizun, take the D764 eastwards, pausing at the Moulins de Kerouat after 3km.

This restored mill complex of bake-houses and outbuildings is now a museum of country life.

Continue on the same road to Commana.

The landscapes become wilder and the hills higher. Commana has a fine church and an *allée couverte*.

East of Commana on the same road is the Roc'h Trévézel.

At 365m, this is one of the best viewpoints in Brittany, with views as far as Lannion Bay on a clear day.

The Moulins de Kerouat once more grind corn

Take the D785 southwards, stopping at Montagne St–Michel after 13km.

This is a slightly higher summit (380m), but it can be reached by car. The surrounding ridge is the highest point in Brittany.

Continue 7km down the D785 to Brasparts.

Brasparts has a fine church and parish close. Inside the church is a lovely baroque altarpiece with blue and gold barleysugar columns decorated with vines and snakes.

Retrace the route for 2.5km northwards and take the D30 northwest to St–Rivoal.

This hamlet has an attractive *ecomusée*, the Maison Cornec. Wind westwards through the lanes to Menez-Meur. This wildlife park and information centre is a good place to put the Armorique Park in perspective.

Return north up the D342 to return to Sizun.

PRESQU'ILE DE CROZON (► 22–23, TOP TEN)

QUIMPER (► 24, TOP TEN)

ROSCOFF ✪✪

Roscoff successfully combines the role of ferry port with that of seaside resort and export centre for vegetables and seafood. Thalassotherapy and seaweed research are other sidelines. The pretty, old fishing quarter remains intact despite the demands of modern shipping. But the picturesquely bereted 'Onion Johnnies' who once loaded their wares on to bicycles for the ferry crossing have long since been replaced by refrigerated container juggernauts. In the old town, the main monument is the church of Notre-Dame-de-Kroaz-Batz, with one of Brittany's finest lantern bell towers. On the Pointe de Bloscon, subtropical gardens flourish in the mild climate. A recommended excursion from Roscoff is the 15-minute boat-trip to the Ile de Batz, a simple island of sandy beaches and seaweed processing – and another splendid exotic garden.

➕ 28B5
🍴 Good choice throughout the town (€–€€€)
🚌 Nos 40 (Brest–Roscoff); 52, 53, or SNCF Line 71 (Morlaix–Roscoff)
⛴ Brittany Ferries terminal; trips to Ile de Batz
ℹ 46 rue Gambetta
☎ 02 98 61 12 13

Roscoff, former hideout of notorious privateers

ST-POL-DE-LÉON ✪✪

During the Middle Ages St-Pol was the religious centre of North Finistère. Its most memorable landmark is the magnificent belfry of the Kreisker Chapel, soaring 77m high. Near by rise the rival twin spires of the Cathedral. Built of sallow Norman limestone, the interior is full of fascinating details. What looks like an old stone bath-tub (a Roman sarcophagus) serves as a stoup, and a little door below the right tower was used by lepers. St-Pol is renowned as an agricultural centre of the immensely fertile Golden Belt (*Ceinture d'Orée*) and all around the town early vegetables grow, particularly onions, artichokes, potatoes and cauliflowers. If you catch it on a Tuesday (market day) you will see it at its liveliest, doing what it does best.

➕ 28B5
🍴 A few eating places in town, such as Auberge Pomme d'Api, 49 rue Verderel (€€)
🚌 Same services as for Roscoff (see above)
ℹ Place de l'Eveché
☎ 02 98 69 05 69

DID YOU KNOW?

In January 1973, a converted tank-landing craft made its first sailing from Roscoff to Plymouth, carrying a consignment of early vegetables. It was quickly dubbed 'The Cauliflower Run'. Within a year, demand for a passenger service grew, and the company now known as Brittany Ferries was launched.

Côtes d'Armor

Few visitors would dispute that the coastline of Côtes d'Armor is the most dramatically beautiful in Brittany. Highlights are the Emerald and Pink Granite coasts, where its northerly peninsulas meet the sea in a spectacular series of headlands, cliffs, bizarre rock formations and scattered islands. Added blessings are its charming old towns (Dinan, Tréguier, Lannion, Paimpol). In summer, its main centres and hotels can become crowded, but nowhere except perhaps St-Brieuc feels overpoweringly urban, and it's never impossible to find a secluded beach. Some areas have fascinating historic associations: the Côte de Goëlo south of Paimpol was a centre of Resistance operations during World War II. Its less well-known interior, startlingly empty in parts, is worth exploring too. As you travel westwards through Côtes d'Armor towards Basse-Bretagne (Lower Brittany), the Breton character becomes steadily more pronounced and Celtic place-names appear on signposts.

> *'Towards the end of each winter, in the port of Paimpol, they received…the parting benedictions…As the boats glided out into the distance, the men sang, in vibrant full-throated voices, the canticles of Marie, Star-of-the-Sea.'*

PIERRE LOTI
Pêcheur d'Islande
1886, translated 1931

Cap Fréhel

What to See in Côtes d'Armor

✚ 29E5

🍽 La Fauconnière (€€)

🚌 CAT Line 02 (from St-Brieuc, Lamballe, Erquy, Le Val-André)

⛴ Boat trips from several Emerald Coast resorts

Phare du Cap Fréhel (lighthouse)

☎ 02 96 41 40 03

🕐 Very irregular access, phone first

♿ None (140 steps)

✋ Free

✚ 29D5–E5

CAP FRÉHEL

This spectacular promontory consists of gnarled grey cliffs of schist and sandstone streaked with red porphyry rising to a height of 70m above a sea of jade. Best views are from the sea; summer excursion boats tour the coast from St-Malo and Dinard. The road approach leads through moorland and pine forests, with parking space at the square-towered **lighthouse**. Views extend to Bréhat, St-Malo and the Channel Isles on clear days, and in misty conditions, a foghorn sounds at intervals. Seabirds crowd on the fissured Fauconnière rocks (a nature reserve).

Walks around the cape, past aged cannons rusting in a froth of sea-pinks and white campion, are exceptionally beautiful. Take binoculars and a camera.

CÔTE D'EMERAUDE ✪✪✪

The Emerald Coast lies between the Pointe de Grouin (north of Cancale), and Le Val-André – a picturesque stretch of rocky headlands, sandy bays, estuaries, capes and islets. The name refers to the lush vegetation on the clifftops rather than the colour of the sea, but sometimes the waves look greenish too. West of St-Malo and Dinard stretches a long string of small resorts, many named after saints and all with lovely sandy beaches – Sables-d'Or-les-Pins and Le Val-André have two of the best. St-Cast-le-Guildo and Le Val-André are the largest and best equipped holiday resorts. East of Cap Fréhel (► above) stands Fort La Latte, a romantic coastal fortress (► 45). The Baie de la Frenaye is renowned for mussel-farming, while Erquy specialises in scallops.

The dramatic red, grey and black cliffs at Cap Fréhel

DID YOU KNOW?

Scenes along the Emerald Coast have inspired many artists, particularly the Impressionists. The region is immortalised in galleries all over the world. An artists' trail called 'Emerald Eyes' follows in their footsteps. Ask the tourist office for a leaflet.

CÔTE DE GRANIT ROSE (► 17, TOP TEN)

DINAN (► 18, TOP TEN)

FORT LA LATTE ✪✪

The romantic setting of this coastal fortress makes it one of the most memorable in Brittany. It stands on a rocky promontory severed from the mainland by chasms forming a natural tidal moat, and is entered by a drawbridge. The present structure dates back mainly to the 14th century, but was extensively renovated by Louis XIV's military architect Vauban at the end of the 17th century. The castle guards the western approach to the Baie de la Frenaye, and has splendid views of the Emerald Coast from its watchtower. During its varied career the castle has played many roles: hosting pirates, English spies, White Russians and latterly, film crews within its pink sandstone ramparts. It is privately owned and still inhabited, but visitors are welcome for guided tours (not obligatory).

ILE DE BRÉHAT ✪✪

This miniature island paradise lies about 2km north of Paimpol. From the mainland it is clearly visible: low-lying and wooded, guarded by a bracelet of half-submerged reefs. Bréhat consists of two main islands linked by a bridge. Beaches of pink granite fringe the indented coastline. The northern island is wilder and less crowded, while the southern island is scattered with elegant villas and subtropical gardens, and contains Bréhat's main community Le Bourg, where in summer the resident population of over 400 swells more than tenfold. Here you can visit the **Moulin à Marée du Birlot**, a restored 17th century windmill. Ferries shuttle to and fro from Pointe de l'Arcouest, hourly in summer, and there are boat excursions from other nearby resorts. The mild, surprisingly dry Gulf Stream climate encourages a great variety of flora and fauna. Cars are banned, but Bréhat is criss-crossed by paths, and small enough to walk or cycle across in an hour.

www.castlelalatte.com
+ 29E5
✉ Plévenon–Fréhel
☎ 02 96 41 40 31
🕓 Easter–Sep 10–12:30, 2:30–6:39; rest of year Sat–Sun & school hols 2–6
♿ None
👆 Moderate

Fort La Latte faces out over the open sea

+ 29D5
🍴 Simple seasonal cafés and restaurants, such as La Potinière, Plage de Guerzido (€€)
🚢 Cruises and ferries from several resorts (Pointe de l'Arcouest, Erquy, Binic, St-Quay-Portrieux)
ℹ La Mairie, Le Bourg
☎ 02 96 20 04 15

Moulin à Marée du Birlot
🕓 Tours: Jun–Aug Sat & Sun PM (depending on tide)
♿ None
👆 Free

45

🚩 29D4

🍴 Restaurants and pubs in old town, such as La Tête Noire, rue du Four (€–€€)

🚌 CAT Lines 01 (St-Cast-le-Guildo), 03 (St-Brieuc)

🚆 SNCF links to Dinan, St-Brieuc, Rennes

ℹ️ Place du Martray

☎ 02 96 31 05 38

❓ Aug: Concours Hippique National (horse championships); Sep: Fête du Cheval (horse festival)

Haras National

✉️ Club Hippique

☎ 02 96 50 06 98

🕐 Mid-Jun to mid-Sep 11–12, 2:30–6 (guided tours; times vary seasonally)

♿ None

💰 Moderate

Musée Mathurin-Méhaut/Musée du Pays de Lamballe et du Penthièvre

✉️ Maison du Bourreau

☎ Musée Mathurin 02 96 31 19 99; Musée du Pays del Lamballe 02 96 31 05 38

🕐 Musée Mathurin: Apr–Sep daily 10–noon, 2:30–5 (until 6 in summer); Oct–Mar Tue, Fri & Sat 2:30–5. Musée du Pays del Lamballe: Sep–Jun daily 10–12:30, 2–6; Jul–Aug Mon–Sat 10–6

♿ None

💰 Inexpensive (joint ticket)

Lamballe's fine half-timbered 15th-century Maison de Bourreau (Executioner's House)

LAMBALLE ⭐⭐

France's second largest **Haras National** (national stud farm) is in the inland town of Lamballe. An imposing

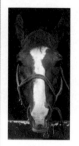

stable-block in extensive grounds just northwest of Lamballe's charming historic centre provides handsome quarters for around 70 stallions, plus a number of riding horses. The most notable breed is the beefy Breton draught horse, once used for ploughing and cart-pulling, but they share their stalls with fine-boned thoroughbreds, saddle horses and Irish Connemaras. Lamballe's social calendar marks several equine events.

Lamballe presides over an agricultural area, and much of its business is related to its role as market centre for the Penthièvre region. It holds large cattle auctions, and has animal foodstuffs and leather processing industries. Modern suburbs sprawl in all directions, but its most attractive part is the old quarter around the place du Martray, a compact cluster of noteworthy churches and picturesque timbered houses. The tourist office occupies one of the most striking of these, the Maison du Bourreau (the Hangman's House). The Maison du Bourreau also houses the **Musée Mathurin-Méhaut**, whilst the **Musée du Pays de Lamballe** is found just beside here at the Hosté du Pilori. One is a local folk and history exhibition; the other displays watercolours, drawings and ceramics by the artist Mathurin Méheut, born in Lamballe in 1882. Lamballe's most interesting churches stand near the main square. St-Jean contains a 17th-century altarpiece and a fine organ; St-Martin is a priory with an unusual canopied porch. The fortified collegiate church of Notre-Dame dominates the upper town with carved portals and a splendid rood-screen.

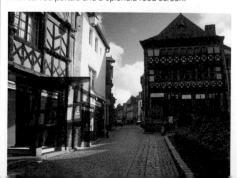

LANNION ★★

This attractive, hilly port straddling the Léguer estuary acts as the administrative centre of the Trégor region. After St-Brieuc, it is the Côtes d'Armor's largest town. A strategic bridging point and route-hub, it gets crowded on market day (Thursday), but is a lively and enjoyable shopping centre. Long wharves and towpaths fringe the waterfront, and fishing boats give the town a seaside air, though it is some distance inland. The lower town is a well-preserved assembly of old gabled houses, some timber-framed and decorated with carvings, others slate-hung with overhanging balconies. Two prominent churches catch the eye on either side of the river: the monastery of Ste-Anne on the west bank and St-Jean-du-Baly in the centre.

Lannion's most interesting church, Brélévenez, crowns the hill to the north of the town and can be reached via a flight of 142 steps, or less arduously by a circuitous road. Founded by 12th-century Templars, it displays a mixture of styles. A stoup by the entrance was used for measuring out tithe wheat. The Romanesque apse is a maze of pillars and ornately carved capitals. The crypt below contains a fine Entombment.

Lannion makes a good excursion base. The Léguer estuary and the wooded valleys inland offer excellent touring. Half a dozen châteaux lie within easy reach, including the stately ruins of Tonquédec and Coatfrec, inhabited Kergrist (gardens open) and richly furnished Rosanbo. Two chapels are worth tracking down. Kerfons has a wonderfully carved rood screen. Les Sept Saints, near Le Run, stands on top of a dolmen and is dedicated to the Seven Sleepers of Ephesus, a band of Christians walled up in a cave for refusing to renounce their faith. They woke miraculously 200 years later.

🔢 28C5

🍴 Cafés and restaurants in old town (€–€€)

🚌 CAT Lines 06 (Guingamp), 07 (Paimpol), 15 (Pink Granite Coast), 16 (Morlaix)

🚊 SNCF Morlaix, Guingamp connections

ℹ️ 2 quai d'Aiguillon
☎ 02 96 46 41 00

❓ Canoeing, kayaking, rafting at the white-water stadium Base Nautique de Lannion
☎ 02 96 37 43 90

A steep flight of steps leads up to the Church of Brélévenz

Drive along the Armorique Corniche

Distance
70km

Time
Allow half a day, with time for a walk or picnic, and a visit to the Cairn de Barnenez

Start point
Lannion
✚ 28C5

End point
Morlaix
✚ 28B5

Lunch
Grand Hôtel des Bains (€€€)
✉ Locquirec
☎ 02 98 67 41 02 (a stylish hotel-restaurant with lovely views) or
Ty Pont (€–€€)
✉ St-Jean-du-Droigt
☎ 02 98 67 34 06 (good-value *Logis*)

The Corniche d'Armorique's Locquirec Bay

This route spans the coastal borderlands of Finistère and Côtes d'Armor, through a landscape of sandy beaches, rocky headlands, fishing ports and estuary scenery.

Take the D786 southwest of Lannion to St–Michel-en-Grève (11km), then detour briefly inland on the D30 to Ploumilliau (4km).

Ploumilliau's 17th-century church contains an unnerving sculpture of Ankou (the Breton representation of Death), ready with scythe and spade to gather in his human crop.

Retrace your route to the D786, and continue westwards along the Lieue de Grève.

St-Michel-en-Grève's beach is a magnificent 4km crescent of firm, perfectly golden sand stretching 2km out to sea at low tide. Sand-yachting is a popular local sport. At the west end of the bay, St-Efflam's chapel has a domed fountain dedicated to the local hermit saint.

Leave the main D786 at St-Efflam and follow the corniche route to Locquirec (D64).

This attractive resort and fishing port occupies a scenic headland where affluent villas take advantage of the views. Just west of the village, more glorious beaches are visible from roadside viewpoints at Marc'h Sammet (good picnic spots on a clear day).

Continue on minor roads, hugging the coast as closely as possible, to St-Jean-du-Droigt.

St Jean-du-Doigt's parish close has a triumphal arch and a beautiful Renaissance fountain in which St John baptises Christ. John the Baptist's index finger was allegedly brought here in the 15th century and is kept in the church.

Take the D46 northwards to Plougasnou, then trickle round more coastal lanes to the Cairn de Barnenez.

Beyond more pretty fishing ports (Le Diben, Térénez) lies the impressive Cairn de Barnenez. This megalithic site of terraced granite has 11 separate burial chambers overlooking the Baie de Morlaix (excellent guided tours).

Continue down the D76 to Morlaix.

PAIMPOL

Paimpol's traditional way of life for centuries was cod-fishing in the perilous waters of Newfoundland and Iceland. Today's trawlers stay closer inshore and oyster-farming in the Trieux estuary has brought new wealth, but the **Musée de la Mer** (Maritime Museum) contains many fascinating reminders of the cod industry. The Place du Martray is the town's focal point. Surrounded by charming old houses, it holds a thriving fish and produce market.

Paimpol lacks good sandy beaches, but makes a fine touring base. Pointe de l'Arcouest (2km north) is the ferry terminal for the Ile de Bréhat (► 45). Southwards lies the Côte de Goëlo, and the impressive ruins of the 13th-century **Abbaye de Beauport** (www.abbaye-beauport. com). A scenic route near Plouha takes in Plage Bonaparte, scene of several daring escapes from occupied France during World War II (clifftop monument). Inland, the church at Kermaria-an-Iskuit contains a *danse macabre* fresco.

🕂 29D5
🍴 Excellent eating places in old town and port (€–€€€)
🚌 CAT Line 09 (St-Brieuc), 07 (Lannion)
ℹ️ Place de la République; ☎ 02 96 20 83 16

Musée de la Mer
✉️ Rue de Labenne
☎ 02 96 22 02 19
🕐 Jun–Aug 10–12, 2:30–6:30; Apr–Sep 2:30–6:30
♿ Good
💷 Moderate

PERROS-GUIREC

The Pink Granite Coast's largest resort is ideal for family holidays. Two splendid beaches, a casino, thalassotherapy centre and modern marina entice many visitors, though the town has no special Breton charm or architectural distinction apart from the church of St-Jacques, with a curious spiky belfry and trefoil porch. Boat trips to the bird sanctuary at Les Sept-Isles are a favourite excursion. Don't miss the watchpath walk to Ploumanac'h past the most spectacular section of the Pink Granite Coast (► 50).

🕂 28C5
🍴 Wide choice (€–€€€)
🚌 CAT Line 15 (Lannion, Trégastel, Trébeurden, Ploumeur-Bodou)
ℹ️ 21 place de l'Hôtel de Ville ☎ 02 96 23 21 15

PLEUMEUR-BODOU

From a distance, a huge white golfball seems to have been abandoned on the heathlands northwest of Lannion. This was once the nerve-centre of France's advanced telecommunications research. In 1962 it received the first transatlantic signals from the American satellite *Telstar*. It now houses the **Musée des Télecoms**, an exhibition on long-distance message-relay from early semaphore to the latest video-telephones. The Radôme show is a high-tech account of satellite communication. The nearby **Planétarium** offers more extraterrestrial experiences (www.leradome.com or www.planetarium-bretagne.fr).

🕂 28C5

Musée des Télecoms/Planétarium
✉️ Site de Cosmopolis
☎ 02 96 46 63 80 (Telecoms); 02 96 15 80 32 (Planétarium)
🕐 Télecoms: Jul–Aug daily 11–9; May–Jun daily 11–6; Apr & Sep Mon–Fri 11–6, Sat–Sun 2–6; shorter hours off-peak. Planétarium: call to check times
🍴 On-site cafés (€)
🚌 CAT Line 15 (Perros-Guirec, Lannion, and Pink Granite resorts)
♿ Good 💷 Moderate

Pleumeur-Bodou's Râdome (radar dome)

A Walk from Perros-Guirec

Distance
6km

Time
About 90min each way

Start
Perros-Guirec
✚ 28C5

End point
Ploumanac'h
✚ 28C5

Lunch
Take a picnic

The coastguard's watchpath by the seashore from Perros-Guirec leads past an astonishing wilderness of rose-tinted boulders weathered into curious shapes. The coppery pink colours are particularly amazing at sunset.

From Perros–Guirec the path begins at Plage de Trestraou, hugging the shore beneath the cliffs.

At first it is pleasant but unspectacular with views of Les Sept-Iles and claw-like headlands. At Pors Rolland the rocks suddenly change gear, revealing weird, organic forms strewn chaotically over the seafront like unclaimed suitcases. The most peculiar of all are located in an orderly conservation zone or 'municipal park', where each formation is given some fanciful name (the Tortoise, the Armchair, etc). At the Maison du Littoral on the edge of the municipal park the emphasis is strictly on environmental care: *'La vie est fragile – ne brisez-la!'* A small display on local geology and natural history is housed inside.

Follow the rocks past the lighthouse right round to Plage St-Guirec, where an oratory and a statue mark the local patron saint.

Oratory of St-Guirec, Ploumanac'h. The saint landed near by in the 6th century

This Celtic monk arrived from Welsh shores in the 6th century and obviously appreciated the scenery. His talents ranged from curing abscesses, retarded children and fiery tempers to an occasional spot of marriage guidance counselling.

In Ploumanac'h, notice the eyecatching Château du Diable, an outcrop of granite rocks in the bay. This is where Heinryk Sienkiewicz wrote Quo Vadis? at the turn of the 20th century. He was awarded the Nobel prize for literature in 1905.

LES SEPT-ILES ✪

The seven scraps of land visible from the coast around Perros-Guirec are one of Brittany's most important bird sanctuaries, home to many species, including petrels and puffins. One island, Rouzic, is noted for a large colony of breeding gannets. Half-day boat trips from Ploumanac'h and Perros-Guirec sail all round the islands. Landings are permitted only on Ile aux Moines, which has a ruined fortress and an old gunpowder factory.

🗺 28C5

✉ Centrale de Réservation Gare Maritime de Perros–Guirec ☎ 02 96 91 10 00 🕐 Feb–Nov

TRÉGASTEL ✪

This popular family resort has some of the strangest of the Pink Granite Coast's rock formations. One extraordinary cluster has been turned into an **aquarium** of local and Mediterranean species (tel: 02 96 23 48 58). Near by, a large indoor waterpark called Forum (tel: 02 96 15 30 44) has several pools maintained at a comfortable 28°C (82°F). Behind is the main beach of Plage de Coz-Pors. More intriguing rocks lie stranded at low tide on Grève Blanche.

🗺 28C5

🍴 Cafés and restaurants near the beaches (€–€€)

🚌 CAT Line 15

ℹ Place St-Anne ☎ 02 96 15 38 38

TRÉGUIER ✪✪

The picturesque historic town of Tréguier occupies a hilly site on the Jaudy estuary. Its most famous resident was Yves, patron saint of lawyers. The cathedral is its most impressive building, a mainly Gothic construction of pink granite. The great spire at its west end is a masterpiece of the Decorated period, pierced with multi-patterned holes to reduce wind resistance. Inside lies St Yves' tomb, flanked by votive candles. On the anniversary of his death on the 19th May, a *pardon* is held. Outside the cathedral lies place du Martray, a wide square surrounded by lovely old houses, some turned into restaurants and shops. Near the tourist office stands a poignant war memorial showing a woman in Breton dress grieving for lost menfolk.

🗺 28C5

🍴 Good choice in old town (€–€€)

🚌 CAT Line 15

ℹ 1 place du Général Leclerc ☎ 02 96 92 22 33

🎉 Mid-May: *Pardon* de St-Yves

Tréguier's splendid pink granite cathedral

In the Know

If you have only a short time to visit Brittany, or would like to get a real flavour of the region, here are some ideas:

10
Ways to Be a Local

Speak some French English is widely spoken in ferry ports and major resorts, but a few words of French are appreciated.

Don't forget greetings and titles Even if you speak no other French, it is courteous to begin any social encounter with a *Bonjour Monsieur* or *Madame*, and take your leave with *Au revoir* and the appropriate title.

Dress appropriately Many Bretons are devout Catholics. Dress discreetly when visiting churches or parish closes, and don't disrupt services or funerals by sightseeing.

Café life Do as the French do, and have coffee in a local café or brasserie, preferably with a copy of *Ouest-France*, Brittany's regional paper.

Don't get drunk But at some point, taste Breton cider. Several regional cider-press museums offer tastings. Local *cervoise* barley beers are worth a try too.

Shop locally Buy picnic or self-catering provisions in specialist shops and markets. Local *pâtisseries*, *boulangeries*, fishmongers and delicatessens are well stocked with biscuits, cakes, cheeses and cooked produce (artichokes, *moules marinières*, etc).

Attend a festival or *pardon* Saints' days, Blessings of the Sea and regional festivals are celebrated all over Brittany, especially in summer. A village *pardon* with a solemn Mass attended by locals in Breton costume is a memorable event.

Find out about Brittany's economy *Ecomusées* give an insight into bygone rural activities in mills, forges, lighthouses etc, but many modern industrial sites can also be visited – such as dockyards, factories, power-stations, fish-farms, seaweed processors.

Take a lunchbreak Many tourists skimp on lunch, but in Brittany, the midday meal is still sacrosanct. Many sights, shops and tourist offices close between noon and 2 or 2:30PM.

Respect the environment Pressure on smaller communities and nature reserves is intense during the tourist season. Be considerate about saving water and energy resources, especially on the islands, and try not to disturb local wildlife.

10
Good Places to Have Lunch

Ar Men Du (€€) Raguenès-Plage, Névez ☎ 02 98 06 84 22 🕒 Easter–Oct. A splendid coastal location overlooking an unspoilt beach and tidal island makes this stylish little restaurant-with-rooms worth finding south of Pont-Aven. Lots of local produce and a friendly welcome.

Auberge du Parc (€€) 162 Ile de Fédrun, St-Joachim ☎ 02 40 88 53 01 🕒 Easter–Oct. Try some of the unusual specialities of the Grande Brière region, such as eel or pike, in this charming thatched house with pretty gardens.

Le Bénétin (€–€€) Les Rochers Sculptés, Rothéneuf ☎ 02 99 56 97 64. This relaxing but sophisticated bar-restaurant and *salon de thé* offers seafood platters with crisp baby vegetables, salads and delicious desserts. Interior décor is stylish enough, but the sea views are rhapsodic.

Le Brittany (€€–€€€) Boulevard Ste-Barbe, Roscoff ☎ 02 98 69 70 78 🕒 Easter–Oct. A lovely manor-house hotel in quiet grounds near the ferry terminal. Its Yachtsman restaurant has wonderful harbour views and notable regional cooking.

La Cigale (€€) 4 place Graslin, Nantes ☎ 02 51 84 94 94 (▶ 98).

Continental (€€) 4 quai Thomas, Cancale ☎ 02 99 89 60 16. One of the best in a bustling parade of seafood restaurants by this famous oyster port. Waterfront views and splendid seafood.

Domaine de la Rochevilaine (€€€) Pointe de Pen Lan, Billiers ☎ 02 97 41 61 61. This luxury hotel is an understandably pricey stay, but lunch in its elegant dining room overlooking the sea may be an affordable treat. Lobster specialities.

La Fauconnière (€€) La Pointe, Cap Fréhel ☎ 02 96 41 54 20 (► 94).

La Ste-Marine (€€–€€€) 19 rue du Bac, Ste-Marine ☎ 02 98 56 34 79. You'd be hard-pressed to find a prettier spot than the terrace of this delightful place overlooking the wooded Odet estuary opposite Bénodet. Very popular; best to book.

Ty Coz (€–€€) Place de l'Eglise, Locronan ☎ 02 98 91 70 79 (► 92).

10

Top Activities

Canal- and river-boating Over 600km of navigable waterways provide an exceptional network, and boats can be hired in many places. Two important waterway junctions are Redon and Dinan.

Canoeing and kayaking Sea, lake and river canoeing is possible in Brittany; several places offer tuition (such as Lannion, Rennes, Mur-de-Bretagne). Choose a millpond or white-water experience.

Cycling Brittany's gentler gradients will appeal to non-masochists, but there's mountain-biking too (► 114).

Fishing Besides being one of Brittany's most important industries, fishing is a recreational activity, from low-tide *pêche-à-pied* with bucket and rake for shellfish to high-tech sport-fishing off the coast.

Brittany's inland waterways provide many opportunities for freshwater angling.

Golf Brittany's golf courses (► 114) range from the exclusive historic links at Dinard to the challengingly designed modern Baden course in Morbihan.

Horse-riding The varied terrain offers a magnificent choice of trekking possibilities (► 114). You can hire a horse-drawn caravan or *roulotte* in the Armorique regional park.

Sailing Brittany's long and varied littoral with its challenging hazards of reefs and currents make it a mecca for keen sailors. The coast is studded with well-equipped marinas (La Forêt-Fouesnant, La Trinité-sur-Mer etc). The sheltered southern waters around Bénodet, Iles de Glénan and Quiberon are ideal places to learn (► 115).

Sand-yachting Also known as sand-karting or landsailing, the landbased windsurfing sport of *char-à-voile* is especially popular on the long, firm strands at Cherreux on Mont-St-Michel Bay, and other parts of the north coast. It's an exciting spectator sport in a high wind (► 115).

Walking Nearly 5,000km of footpaths make walking Brittany's most popular recreational activity. Coastal walks, canal towpaths and forest trails cater for all fitness levels, but there are three challenging *Grandes Randonnées* (long-distance footpaths) too (► 114).

Watersports Surfing, windsurfing and scuba-diving are available in many resorts all around the coast. Most cater for beginners and experts. Underwater photography courses and wreck-diving are specialist activities (► 115).

10

Top Parish Closes

- **Brasparts** (► 40) has a fine calvary depicting St Michael slaying a dragon.
- **Guéhenno** This charmingly naïve calvary was damaged in the Revolution, and restored by the local priest. The cock symbolises Peter's denial of Christ.
- **Guimiliau** (► 20, Top Ten).
- **La Martyre** An ancient parish close with an interesting ossuary and triumphal door. Extensive interior decoration.
- **Pencran** A 16th-century ossuary, carved porch and balconied belfry distinguish this church.
- **Pleyben** Very large calvary and handsome church interior (carved beams and altarpieces).
- **Plougastel-Daoulas** A large, elaborate calvary and plague cross. Carvings of Catell Gollet (► 20).
- **La Roche-Maurice** A classical ossuary with an Ankou figure of death, and twin-galleried belfry. Lovely Renaissance rood screen in the church.
- **St-Thégonnec** A fine calvary and triumphal arch, and splendid church interior too. Notice the local saint with his tame wolf.
- **Sizun** (► 40) This church has a triumphal arch and a 16th-century ossuary, with rich panelling inside the church.

5

Top Fortresses

- **Combourg** (► 56)
- **Fougères** (► 19)
- **Josselln** (► 85)
- **Nantes** (► 76–77)
- **Vitré** (► 66)

Ille-et-Vilaine

This easterly *département* in Haute-Bretagne has two of Brittany's best-known towns: the popular ferry port of St-Malo, and the stylish resort of Dinard. It has hardly any of Brittany's rugged coastline, yet is by no means devoid of scenery and sightseeing. Don't miss the grand fortresses of Fougères, Combourg and Vitré that once protected the independent Duchy from its jealous French sister. The Breton capital, Rennes, deserves a day or two's exploration. And slip briefly across the Norman border for a look at one of France's greatest sights, the island abbey of Mont-St-Michel.

The brief stretch of coast between the Rance and Normandy consists of flat, brackish saltmarshes. Southwards carve the sluggish waterways that give the *département* its name, linking the Channel with the Atlantic and saving fair-weather sailors the anxiety of negotiating Finistère's treacherous coastline.

> '*Close to his ear he could hear, issuing from the creels, the moist susurrus of a fistful of shrimps and the sharp scraping of a large crab's claw against the lid.* '

SIDONIE GABRIELLE COLETTE,
Le Blé en Herbe, 1923, translated as *The Ripening Seed*, 1955

Plage de l'Ecuse, Dinard's main beach

What to See in Ille-et-Vilaine

CANCALE ✪✪

Cancale is renowned for its oysters. The grey shoreline is covered with the shallow concrete beds (*parcs*) where they mature. After harvesting and cleaning, they are piled high on local stalls, or more expensively, at the colourful seafood restaurants all along the waterfront in the picturesque port of La Houle.

Just south of the port lies **La Ferme Marine**, an oyster farm and museum devoted to the life and times of the local mollusc (guided tours). After an introductory film-show, visitors are shown the oyster-beds and the workshops where washing, grading and packing take place. An elegantly restored *bisquine* (oyster boat) now used for pleasure trips recalls the days when local fishermen trawled the sea-bed for wild oysters.

COMBOURG ✪✪

The massive 11th-century castle by the lakeshore, all crenellations and pepperpot towers, is the main focus of attention in this small town. Literary visitors have an additional interest in the building. The castle was the family home of the writer René de Chateaubriand, who wrote vividly of his miserable childhood in the haunted bedroom. The old town is attractive, though a traffic bottleneck.

The pepper-pot towers of Combourg's castle pierce the surrounding trees

---

✚ 29E5

🍴 Seafood restaurants at the port; Maisons de Bricourt restaurants (€–€€€)

🚌 St-Malo–Mont-St-Michel

ℹ 44 rue du Port

☎ 02 99 89 63 72

La Ferme Marine

✉ Plage de l'Aurore

☎ 02 99 89 69 99

🕑 Jun–Sep, tours daily 2 (English); mid-Feb–Oct Mon–Fri 3 (French only)

✋ Moderate

✚ 29E4

🍴 Nearby hotel-restaurants Du Château and Du Lac, place Chateaubriand, or restaurant L'Ecrivain, near the church on place St-Gilduin (€€)

🚌 SNCF (St-Malo–Rennes)

ℹ Place Albert Parent
☎ 02 99 73 13 93

Château de Combourg

✉ 23 rue des Princes

☎ 02 99 73 22 95; www.combourg.net

🕑 Apr–Jun, Sep–Oct 2–5:30; Jul–Aug daily 11–5:30 (guided tours). Closed Sat off-peak. Park: Apr–Oct 9–12, 2–6

♿ None

✋ Moderate

DINARD ✪✪

This fashionable seaside resort was a mere fishing village until the mid-19th century. The sheltered climate and beautiful setting attracted wealthy visitors who built large ornate villas on the wooded cliffs above three sandy beaches (best admired from the Promenade du Clair-de-Lune). Holiday homes, smart yachts and striped beach-huts jostle along the seafront. Dinard's excellent facilities include an Olympic-sized swimming pool, a casino, the modern Palais des Arts et Festivals and boat trips up the Rance and along the Emerald Coast. Regattas, tennis tournaments, bridge and afternoon tea punctuate the social calendar. On the Rance estuary just south of Dinard is the world's first tidal power station (➤ 65), a dam which doubles as a road-bridge connection to St-Malo.

🕂 29E5
🍴 Wide choice (€–€€€)
▢ TIV (St-Malo–Emerald Coast)
⛴ Ferry to St-Malo; Rance cruises to Dinan; coastal trips
ℹ 2 boulevard Féart
☎ 02 99 46 94 12

DOL-DE-BRETAGNE ✪✪

Dol stands on the remains of a cliff amid low-lying pastureland reclaimed from the sea. The surrounding fields are famous for the prized *pré-salé* lamb raised here. Dol was founded in the 6th century by St Samson, one of Brittany's 'founding saints'. Its gaunt granite cathedral still dominates the town. A former school beside the cathedral houses an ambitious exhibition on medieval cathedrals, and the construction methods used during the period, called **Cathédraloscope**. The explanatory labels to the models, diagrams and photographs have been translated into English but are rather technical. Several streets of picturesque timbered houses dating from the Middle Ages lie nearby.

Just north of the town, the Mont-Dol, a granite mound topped by an ancient chapel, erupts suddenly from the saltmarsh plains, offering extensive views of the surrounding countryside. A legend declares this is the site of St Michael's apocalyptic struggle with Satan, and if you let your imagination run away with you, it is possible to spot St Michael's footprint in a clifftop rock by the chapel.

🕂 29E4
🍴 Pleasant eating places in old town (€–€€); windmill *crêperie* Le Moulin du Mont, Mont-Dol (€–€€)
▢ Mont St-Michel–Dol
🚉 SNCF (Caen, Dinan, St-Malo, Rennes connections)
ℹ Place de la Cathédrale
☎ 02 99 48 15 37

Cathédraloscope
✉ Place de la Cathédrale
☎ 02 99 48 35 30
🕐 Apr–Oct daily 10–7; Feb–Mar, Nov–Dec groups only
♿ Good
🎗 Moderate

Fishermen at Cancale

29F4

Restaurants and cafés in upper town, such as Les Voyageurs, 10 place Gambetta, or in old quarter around castle (€–€€)

Regular bus and coach services from Rennes, St-Malo, Vitré

1 place Aristide Briand
☎ 02 99 94 12 20

Vitré (➤ 66)

View over Fougères from the Public Gardens

FOUGÈRES

Fougères is a frontier town, former capital of the swampy Marches dividing France and Brittany. Duchess Anne dubbed it 'the key to my royal treasure'; for Victor-Hugo Fougères was 'the Carcassonne of the North'. Its dominant feature is its castle (➤ 19, Top Ten), set in a tight loop of the River Nançon. The rocky spurs above the castle walls cradle the upper town of mostly 18th-century buildings – a stiff climb from the riverbank. Precipitous steps and alleys lead from the back of St-Léonard's church down to a much older sector around the place du Marchix, where tanneries and mills can be seen among an enchanting cluster of stone and half-timbered 16th-century houses, dominated by the slender spire of St-Sulpice.

Fougères grew wealthy, like many Breton towns, on the textile trades of wool and hemp. Later it turned its ancient cattle market and tanning business to good use in shoe manufacture, supplemented by post-war ventures into electronics and robotics. Northeast of Fougères, beyond uninspiring modern suburbs, extends a state forest of beech, spruce and chestnut.

29E4

Charming restaurants in quaint buildings, such as La Vieille Auberge, Hostellerie du Vieux Moulin, Le Genty Home (all on route de Tinténiac, €€)

On Rennes–St-Malo route

La Mairie
☎ 02 99 45 46 18

HÉDÉ

Woods and water are the lasting impressions of this hill village. Streams, cascades and ponds gleam all around, and lush, terraced gardens almost hide the crumbling stone houses and castle ruins perched on an outcrop of rock. In the churchyard, bronze memorials commemorate fallen war heroes.

Just north of the village at La Madeleine, the Ille-et-Rance canal passes through a magnificent staircase of 11 locks. The towpath walk is pleasant, though overgrown in places. A small exhibition about the Ille-et-Rance canal stands near the locks.

Walk around the old town of Fougères

Head for the upper town and park in one of the squares near the tourist office. From here, walk along the pedestrianised rue Nationale.

Notice the elegant 14th-century belfry behind the covered market. Further along, a picturesque jettied and porticoed 16th-century house contains a museum dedicated to the Impressionist painter Emmanuel de la Villéon (1858–1944), a native of Fougères. About 60 of his drawings and watercolours (mostly local scenes) are displayed inside. Near the end of the street stands the church of St-Léonard by the Renaissance town hall. Behind the church, which dates from the 16th century, neatly kept municipal gardens give a splendid terrace vantage point over plunging wooded chasms, the mellow, brown-beamed houses of the Marchix quarter and the tremendous fortress below.

Using these as your target, thread your way down the stepped alleys and across the river via the rue des Tanneurs.

The streets around the place du Marchix contain many ancient buildings. Gothic St-Sulpice church, built in Flamboyant style, contains fine 18th-century woodwork, 15th-century granite altarpieces and a charming 12th-century statue of the Virgin Mary (Notre-Dame-des-Marais) suckling a Child who looks well past weaning age.

Visit the castle
(➤ 19) next, but take a walk outside the walls for an impressive overview before going inside. Walk the ramparts.

Notice the foundations of the keep (destroyed in 1166), and the waterwheels by the gatehouse.

Return to the upper town via rue de la Pinterie, a steep climb. More gardens halfway up the hill offer a chance to catch your breath, and a final panorama of the castle and river.

Distance
3km (very hilly! – a *petit train* will spare your legs if you can't face the final climb)

Time
Allow half a day with time to look round the sights

Start/end point
The tourist office in the upper town (place Aristide Briand)
✚ 29F4

Lunch
Les Voyageurs (€–€€)
✉ 10 place Gambetta (100m E of tourist office)
☎ 02 99 99 28 89
or
Le Mediéval (€–€€)
(simple terrace dining beside the castle moat)
☎ 02 99 94 92 59

The north front and tower of the Church of St-Léonard, situated in a wide loop of the River Nançon

29E4

Menhir de Champ-Dolent, fashioned from local granite

MENHIR DE CHAMP-DOLENT ✪

Just southeast of Dol-de-Bretagne, off the D795, is a large, single standing stone about 9m high, stuck incongruously in a maize field. The menhir is alleged to have fallen from heaven to divide the armies of two warring brothers (Champ Dolent means 'Field of Sorrow'). It is said to be gradually sinking into the ground a couple of centimetres every century, and when it vanishes the world will end. The stone is freely accessible near the road, and can even be admired from a picnic table, though it has no markings or particular features of interest.

REDON ✪✪

This attractive flower-filled town is an important junction: roads, railways, waterways and regional boundaries converge here. The Nantes–Brest Canal crosses the Vilaine at this point, joining the Oust to the north of the town. Ille-et-Vilaine, Morbihan and Loire-Atlantique meet on Redon's doorstep, and six major roads intersect. When the River Vilaine was fully navigable, Redon was a significant inland port. The elegant homes of former shipowners line the waterfront and parts of the old town. Today, river access to the south coast is blocked by the Arzal dam near La Roche-Bernard, but pleasure craft ply the local waterways in great numbers, negotiating Redon via a complicated series of locks.

The Grande Rue is one of its finest streets, full of splendid stone and half-timbered buildings decked with bright window-boxes.

 29E2

🍽 Good choice in town centre and port, including some high-quality dining, such as Jean-Marc Chandouineau, 10 avenue de la Gare (€€€)

🚌 TIM Line 10 (La Gacilly–Rochefort-en-Terre)

🚆 SNCF (connections to Rennes, Vannes and Nantes)

⛴ River and canal cruises along the Oust and down the Vilaine to the Arzal dam; boat hire

ℹ Place de la République ☎ 02 99 71 06 04

❓ Fête de Teillouse (a chestnut festival and gastronomic fair, late Oct)

> ### DID YOU KNOW?
>
> The cosmetics empire of Yves Rocher is based in the pretty craft village of La Gacilly (16km north of Redon). Visitors are welcome to watch the manufacturing processes (based on natural rather than synthetic materials) and buy beauty products.
> The Végétarium is a fascinating exhibition about the world of plants and their uses.

Above and right: *Pleasure craft ply Redon's waterways, at the junction of the River Vilaine and the Nantes-Brest Canal*

Redon's main landmark is the church of St-Sauveur, a curious mixture of styles. A Romanesque lantern tower sits unexpectedly on Gothic buttressing, with a separate bell tower nearby. The **Musée de la Batellerie** charts the history of the port and its waterborne trade. Redon makes an enjoyable excursion base for a day or two, with useful hotels and some excellent restaurants. You can hire bikes, canoes or canal boats from numerous outlets in the town and port. In late autumn, the chestnut forests on the outskirts of town take centre stage in a festival called the Fête de Teillouse. During the October harvest, local restaurants compete to produce chestnut-based dishes – its terrines are justly renowned.

The quiet moorland around St-Just, about 18km northeast of Redon, is sprinkled with neolithic monuments. The standing stones and dolmens at Landes de Cojoux and Croix St-Pierre can be freely explored (summer weekend guided tours in French only from St-Just).

Musée de la Batellerie
Quai Jean-Bart
02 99 72 30 95
Jun–mid-Sep daily 10–12, 3–6; Mon, Wed & weekends 2–6 off-peak
Few
Inexpensive

61

29E3

Excellent choice in central areas (€–€€€)

The new Métro is mainly geared towards commuter travel; useful if you're staying in the suburbs

Major route-hub for inter-urban and local services throughout Brittany; many local buses

National TGV and regional services throughout Brittany

International and domestic flights (Air France/Brit'Air)

11 rue St-Yves
☎ 02 99 67 11 11

RENNES ✪✪

Rennes is a burgeoning industrial and academic centre with a cosmopolitan air. Its inland location amid low-lying, humdrum scenery entices comparatively few holiday-makers from the coastal areas, but it is well worth a day's excursion. Driving and parking in the city centre can be difficult, but Rennes is well served by public transport from most Breton cities. The central sights are compact and can easily be explored on foot. Nightlife is lively, especially in the old quarter during term-time when students pack its bars and restaurants. During July, Rennes hosts a major arts festival called Les Tombées de la Nuit (www. ville-rennes.fr), where rock and jazz fans congregate.

The city developed in Roman times from a Gaulish settlement. It soon became a strategic route-hub, the Breton capital in 1562, and played a leading role in Brittany's struggle to retain an independent voice after unification with France. It remains a focus of separatist sentiments. In 1720 disaster struck when a drunken carpenter accidentally started a fire in the old town; it

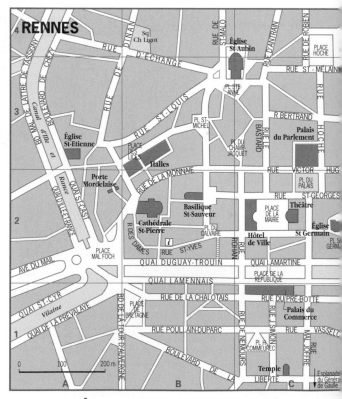

burned for nearly a week. The charred centre was rebuilt in a chilly neo-classical style. Today, examples of this grand civic architecture stand alongside the medieval buildings that survived the fire. In a second mishap, the **Palais du Parlement** (Breton Parliament) was badly damaged during fish-price riots in 1994. It has now been restored to its former glory (guided tours, tel: 02 99 67 11 11). The Hôtel de Ville (town hall) dominates the place de la Marie. St-Pierre, Rennes' cathedral, is a relatively undistinguished 19th-century building containing a fine Flemish altarpiece. East of the old town, the peaceful Jardin du Thabor was once the garden of the Benedictine abbey of St-Melaine.

Rennes has several excellent museums. The **Musée des Beaux-Arts** has an important collection, including works by the Pont-Aven School (➤ 39). The **Musée de Bretagne** (in the same complex but due to move to the Nouvel Espace Culturel) is undergoing reorganisation and is open only for temporary exhibitions. Southeast, at Ferme de la Bintinais, the **Ecomusée du Pays de Rennes** traces the evolution of agricultural life in Brittany from the 16th century.

Musée des Beaux-Arts
- ✉ 20 quai Emile Zola
- ☎ 02 99 28 55 85
- 🕐 All year 10–12, 2–6. Closed Tue & hols
- ♿ Good 👐 Moderate
- Ⓜ République

Musée de Bretagne
- ☎ 02 99 28 55 84
- ♿ Good 👐 Variable

Ecomusée du Pays de Rennes
- ☎ 02 99 51 38 15
- 🕐 Apr–Sep Tue–Sun 9–6; Oct–Mar Tue–Fri 9–12, 2–6, Sat 2–6, Sun 2–7. Closed Mon & hols
- ♿ Few 👐 Moderate
- 🚌 Lines 14, 61 from centre

Rennes' old town

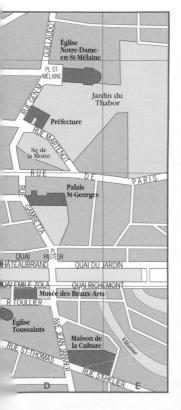

Walk around the old town of Rennes

Distance
3.5km

Time
Half a day, including visiting the main sights

Start point
Hôtel de Ville
✠ 62C2

End point
Musée des Beaux-Arts
✠ 63D1

Lunch
Lots of choice en route, such as Crêperie Sainte-Anne (€)
✉ 5 place Ste-Anne
☎ 02 99 79 22 72 (one of the best *crêperies* in Rennes)

The Tabor Gardens – once the orchards of a former Benedictine abbey

Start in place de la Mairie by the imposing Hôtel de Ville.

This building with its huge clocktower is one of Jacques Gabriel's most confident municipal statements after the great fire of 1720 (free guided tours). Opposite stands a charmingly ornate theatre.

Head west along rue Du Guesclin then north along rue Clisson and west again along rue de la Monnaie.

Notice the rococo-style church of St-Sauveur. Our Lady of Miracles saved Rennes from the English in 1357. Marble plaques thank her for latterday favours, including success in exams. The cathedral of St-Pierre, a 19th-century building in Roman style, contains a splendid Flemish altarpiece in a side chapel. Find the light-switch to enjoy its amazing 3-D effects.

Thread through a quaint maze of streets lined with picturesque houses south of the cathedral, then north via rue des Dames.

The Porte-Mordelaise is the last remnant of the 15th-century ramparts, through which the dukes of Brittany passed for their coronations.

Head northeast through the place des Lices.

Medieval jousts were held in this fine old square. The art nouveau *halles* (covered market) dates from 1622.

Pass through place St–Michel and place Ste–Anne, head south via place du Champ Jacquet, then east along rue la Fayette and rue Nationale to the place du Parlement de Bretagne.

The tall, stripy buildings in place du Champ Jacquet are 17th-century, predating the Great Fire. Brittany's restored Parliament building makes an impressive statement on a spacious square of orderly gardens.

Head east along rue Victor Hugo, north up rue Général M Guillaudot and through the Jardin du Thabor via place St–Melaine. Finish the walk on the south bank of the river, at the museum complex (quai Emile Zola).

LA ROCHE AUX FÉES ✪✪

✚ 29F3

Stranded way inland some 15km west of La Guerche-de-Bretagne, La Roche aux Fées attracts far fewer visitors than Carnac or Locmariaquer. It is, however, a most impressive megalithic monument, consisting of 42 slabs of mauve schist carefully balanced into what looks like an *allée couverte* or gallery grave high enough to walk upright inside (freely accessible). There is much speculation about its age and origins. Traditionally, engaged couples come here and separately count the stones. If they agree on the number, a happy future is presaged.

La Roche aux Fées is one of Brittany's largest megalithic monuments

ST-MALO (▶ 25, TOP TEN)

USINE MARÉMOTRICE DE LA RANCE ✪✪

A huge concrete barrage blocks the mouth of the Rance, creating a large reservoir upstream, and used as a bridge by the St-Malo–Dinard road. From parking places at either end, walkways lead across the dam, from which you can watch sinewy torrents racing through the sluice gates with colossal force to the generators beneath. You can visit the internal workings of the power station via the visitor centre on the Dinard side, and learn lots of technical details.

The dam was first opened in 1967, and spans 750m, curbing a reservoir of 22sq km. A lock surmounted by a swing-bridge enables sizeable boats to pass through. The 24 generators housed in a vast tunnel within the barrage generate over 600 million kWh a year, using both ebb and flow tides. However, this massively imaginative and costly project generates only about 3 per cent of Brittany's total electricity needs, and although it sounds environmentally friendly, its effects on local wildlife are significant.

✚ 29E5
✉ La Richardais
☎ 02 99 16 37 14
🕐 Fri 1–7 (daily during school hols)
🚌 CAT Line 14 (St-Malo–Dinard)
⛴ Rance cruises; ferry (St-Malo–Dinard)
♿ Good
🖐 Free

65

+ 29F3

🍴 Attractive eating places all through the old town (€–€€€)

🚌 SNCF coach line 74 (Fougères); connections to Rennes via Châteaubourg

🚆 SNCF connections to Rennes and Normandy

ℹ Place Charles-de-Gaulle
☎ 02 99 75 04 46

Château/museums

✉ Place du Château
☎ 02 99 75 04 54
🕐 Apr–Jun daily 10–12, 2–5:30; Jul–Sep daily 10–6; Oct–Mar Wed–Fri 10–12, 2–5:30, Sat–Mon 2–5:30
♿ None
💰 Moderate (a museum pass gives combined entrance to all Vitré's museums and the Château des Rochers-Sevigné)
❓ Night tours organised by the tourist office www.ot-vitre.fr

Vitré's imposing triangular château in the old quarter

VITRÉ ●●

The silhouette of old Vitré makes a striking impact on the skyline, best seen from the Fougères road. After Dinan, it is perhaps Brittany's best-preserved medieval town. Close to the town, a hilly belvedere by the banks of the Vilaine, called the Tertres Noires, gives a splendid view of its bristling turrets, drum towers and ramparts. This formidable **château** dates mainly from the 13th century, but was much enlarged and modified during the 16th and restored after years of neglect in the late 19th century. Vitré's strategic location on the borders between France and Brittany made it a constant target during the struggles of the Middle Ages. Today the castle houses several small **museums**, including a startling assembly of natural history specimens.

The delightful old town stretches through cobbled hilly streets below the castle, its half-timbered, slate-hung houses splaying in all directions; some are now tastefully converted into shops and restaurants. Best are those along rue de la Baudrairie, Vitré's former leather-working quarter. The town attracts many visitors and much of its revenue now springs from tourism, though in former centuries its prosperity came mostly from the textile trade (hemp, sailcloth, wool and hosiery). Many wealthy merchants settled in the town and built fine mansions that have given Vitré a lasting touch of class. Henri IV paid the town a famous compliment several hundred years ago: 'Were I not King of France, I would be a citizen of Vitré.'

Notre-Dame church has an exterior pulpit, from which its Catholic incumbent regaled the Protestant Huguenot families who lived opposite. Southeast of Vitré stands Madame de Sevigné's former home, the Château des Rochers-Sevigné.

An Excursion to Mont-St-Michel

The fickle course of the River Couesnant (the Norman boundary) now deprives Brittany by a hair's breadth of one of France's most evocative sights. The abbey-crowned island of Mont-St-Michel tapers mirage-like above the swirling mudflats of the bay. A golden statue of the Archangel Michael is poised on its topmost spire. It attracts more visitors than anywhere else in provincial France. Once in a lifetime, at least, everyone should see it.

Arrive early to beat the crowds (preferably before 9AM when the abbey opens). Drive across the causeway, and park beside it, taking careful note of the tide tables (parts of the car-park flood at high tide). Enter the island near the tourist office, and collect a plan of the site. Make your way up the steep, narrow Grande Rue, lined with souvenir shops and cafés.

The touristy village at the base of the Mount may be off-putting, but the medieval buildings are undeniably quaint. Soon the crowds thin out and the atmosphere becomes much more peaceful. Flights of steps lead everywhere, and it's a steep climb. Several little museums can be visited on the way to the abbey. The Musée de la Mer is an exhibition about the bay and its exceptional tides, which race across the flat sands faster than a horse can gallop (or so it is claimed). Next is the Archéoscope, an archangelic multimedia presentation about the abbey (St Michael is your guide). Still further up near the parish church is Tiphaine's House, built by the medieval warrior Bertrand Du Guesclin (then commander of the Mount) for his scholarly wife in 1365.

Continue up the hill and enter the abbey.

The abbey is a masterpiece of Romanesque and Gothic architecture. Founded in 708 by the Bishop of Avranches, it has been a place of pilgrimage for over a thousand years. Known as La Merveille (The Marvel), it seems as delicately balanced as a house of cards, some sections cantilevered over thin air, others tightly buttressed to the living granite. Beyond the church, a signed route leads through the refectory, cloisters and Knights' Hall down into the crypt.

After visiting the interior, take a walk around the ramparts and gardens for a breathtaking overview of the abbey and the bay.

🚹 29F5

☎ Abbey 02 33 89 80 00; www.mt.st.michel.com

🕐 May–Aug daily 9–6; Sep–Apr 9:30–5 (abbey church service at 12:15)

🍴 Cafés and restaurants in the village; best known is La Mère Poulard (€–€€€) Grande Rue ☎ 02 33 60 14 01 or its sibling Les Terrasses Poulard (€€) directly opposite (terrific views; omelettes are the house speciality)

🚌 Line 30 (St-Malo); many excursion buses

♿ Not suitable (steep steps everywhere)

🎫 No charge to visit the Mount but parking and sights expensive. Abbey ticket price includes a choice of self-guided, escorted or audio-tour; individual or combined tickets available for the museums

The unmistakable silhouette of Mont-St-Michel

Loire-Atlantique

In 1973, Brittany's southeastern wing was torn away to form part of a neighbouring region, Pays-de-la-Loire. But for many Bretons, the natural boundary of Brittany is still the final reach of the River Loire. In this book, Loire-Atlantique is treated as part of Brittany, at least as far as that great southern moat.

The beaches are among Brittany's best. Besides the magnificent crescent of sand at La Baule, or Monsieur Hulot's holiday beach at St-Marc, there are many unspoilt hideaways. Nature-lovers will enjoy the fascinating boglands of La Grande Brière, now a regional park, and the strange saltmarshes of Guérande.

Inland, Loire-Atlantique has fine border castles at Ancenis, Châteaubriant and Grand-Fougeray. The waterways around Nantes and the canals of La Grande Brière suggest interesting boat trips. Highlight of this *département*, though, is the city of Nantes, Brittany's former capital and one of France's liveliest provincial centres.

> *'God's teeth, they are no small beer, these Dukes of Brittany!'*

HENRI IV, KING OF FRANCE,
on first seeing the château at
Nantes when visiting the city in
1598 to sign the Edict of
Nantes

———————————————●———————————————

Beach at La Baule

What to See in Loire-Atlantique

BATZ-SUR-MER ✪✪

At Batz, the low-lying saltmarshes are interrupted by the 60m pepperpot tower of St-Guénolé, a prominent land- and seamark (climbable – excellent views). The chancel is draped with fishing nets, a reminder of its seafaring patronage. The ruined chapel behind St-Guénolé is Notre-Dame-du-Mûrier (Our Lady of the Mulberry Tree), legendarily built by a 15th-century nobleman, saved from shipwreck by the light of a miraculous burning tree. In rue Pasteur is the **Musée des Marais Salants** (Saltmarsh Museum; tel: 02 40 23 82 79), a fascinating exhibition about the local salt industry. On the coast road to Le Pouliguen, **Le Grand Blockhaus** re-creates life in a World War II German command post in one of the biggest concrete bunkers of the Atlantic Wall (tel: 02 40 23 88 29).

LA BAULE ✪✪

La Baule is one of the smartest and largest resorts in northern France, packed at weekends with affluent sophisticates from Paris and other cities, yet it dates back barely a century. The low-lying seafront, periodically engulfed in Loire silt and shifting sands, supported a single fishing village, Escoublac, until 1840, when pine trees were planted to stabilise the dunes and act as a windbreak. In 1879, after the arrival of the railway, the first holiday developments began to appear.

A 5km beach of gleaming golden sand is its main attraction, shelving so gently that you can safely wade far out to sea. Apartment blocks and large hotels line the seafront road, some awesomely grand, most charmlessly modern and boxlike. Behind lie tree-lined avenues of seemly villas dating from a more gracious *belle époque* age. The marina at Le Pouliguen is full of elegant craft.

La Baule offers every kind of seaside diversion, from genteel pursuits like bridge and golf to a casino and the latest high-tech watersports and thalassotherapy. The streets near place de la Victoire bristle with up-market shops and restaurants, and during the season the social diary is never empty.

29D2

🍴 Simple *crêperies* and cafés in resort. On bay road, L'Atlantide (€€)
✉ Plage St-Michel
☎ 02 40 23 91 92 or
L'Ecume de Mer (€€)
✉ Route de la Grande Côte ☎ 02 40 23 91 40 (good seafood)

🚌 Réseau Atlantic Line 81 (Le Croisic–La Baule)

ℹ 25 rue de la Plage
☎ 02 40 23 92 36

29E2

🍴 Wide choice throughout the resort (€–€€€)

🚌 Réseau Atlantic Lines 81 (Le Croisic–St-Nazaire), 82, 83 (Pornichet–St-Nazaire), 83 (Guérande–St-Nazaire); *petit train* along seafront to Pornichet

🚆 Regular TGV connections with Paris

ℹ 8 place de la Victoire
☎ 02 40 24 34 44
www.labaule.fr

CHÂTEAUBRIANT ✪

Set well inland amid lake-strewn woodland, Châteaubriant stands guard on the Anjou border, part of the line of fortified bastions protecting Brittany from invasion. Its red sandstone church, St-Jean-de-Béré, dates back to the 11th century; its altarpieces are mostly 17th century. The main landmark is the castle, a piecemeal structure, partly feudal, partly Renaissance. The keep is the oldest section; the Seigneurial Palace was built by Jean de Laval, Count of Châteaubriant. A balcony at the top of the central staircase overlooks the gardens of the Court of Honour and the rest of the castle.

➕ 29F3

🍽 Restaurants on outskirts; simple eating places near castle, such as Le Bilig (€)
  ✉ Place St-Nicolas
  ☎ 02 40 81 48 49

🚆 SNCF connections with Rennes and Nantes

ℹ 22 rue de Couéré
  ☎ 02 40 28 20 90

Chateaubriant's handsome castle

Château de Châteaubriant

✉ Rue du Château
☎ 02 40 28 20 20
🕐 Mid-Jun to mid-Sep 10–12:15, 2–6:30; mid-Sep to mid-Jun 2–5. Closed Tue
♿ None
💰 Moderate

Food & Drink

Brittany produces an enviable range of high-quality foodstuffs. Regional dishes make good use of seafood, pork and prime vegetables, but Bretons have a sweet tooth too, and love puddings and biscuits. Filled pancakes are a ubiquitous speciality.

Brittany is justly renowned for its outstanding seafood

Seafood
Brittany is one of France's foremost fishing regions, and its seafood predictably superb. Visit a *criée* (fish auction) or fish farm for some idea of this marine cornucopoia. If you don't enjoy seafood much, you may be unable to look another *assiette de fruits de mer* in the eye by the end of your visit. These platefuls of seaweed and crushed ice, piled high with curious sea-creatures, can be a daunting sight. Most include mussels or oysters (prime local products). Winkles, crayfish, clams, crabs and scallops may also put in an appearance. If you prefer your fish hot, try a traditional Breton *cotriade*, or fish stew, somewhat less spicy than a *bouillabaisse*. Look out for freshwater species, especially in the Brière region. *Brochet beurre blanc* is a classic pike dish in Nantais white butter sauce. Most Breton of all, though, is the lobster, often prepared in a sauce of tomato, garlic, shallots and cognac (*homard à l'armoricaine*). On many menus it appears as *homard à l'américaine*, often attributed to a spelling mistake in a Parisian restaurant.

A Recipe for *Far Breton*
Ingredients: 125g plain wheat flour; 4 eggs; 125g sugar; 750ml milk; 250g prunes, 2tbsp rum, 2 sachets of vanilla sugar; a pinch of salt.
Preheat oven (240°C/465°F/gas mark 8). Sift flour into a basin and add sugar, salt and vanilla sugar; make a well and add the eggs. Stir to a smooth paste. Heat the milk with the rum and prunes. Add to the paste and mix vigorously. Pour the batter into a buttered dish and bake for 10 minutes, then reduce to 200°C/390°F/gas mark 6 for 30 minutes until well browned. Serve warm. As a variation, substitute dried apricots, sultanas or fresh cherries for the prunes.

Meat and Poultry
Steak Chateaubriand is the most widely known Breton meat dish. But Brittany is more famous for its dairy produce than its beef. More typical meat products include the distinctively flavoured *pré salé* (salt meadow) lambs raised on the saltmarshes of Ouessant and Mont-St-Michel. *Gigot à la bretonne* (roast leg of lamb with haricot beans) is a local speciality. Brittany produces vast quantities of pork, and *charcuterie* takes many forms – especially sausages, black puddings and *andouille*, a sort of pork haggis not to everyone's taste. Hearty peasant soups

and casseroles like *Kig-ha-Farz* often contain ham or bacon. Some of France's most succulent chickens come from around Rennes, while the *challan* is a delicious duck from the Nantes region.

Pancakes

Once, pancakes were a staple diet in Brittany, replacing bread in poor homes. You will find *crêperies* everywhere – a cheap, quick and filling way of satisfying hunger pangs, and a good choice for vegetarians. You can eat pancakes standing up at a market stall cheaply – great for the entertainment value of watching them being made. The variety of fillings offered is imaginative, but the more exotic the filling, the more it will cost.

Two kinds are made: *crêpes* and *galettes*. Generally, *crêpes* are made with a wheat-flour batter, and have sweet fillings. The more traditional *galettes* are made with heavier buckwheat flour and are generally savoury. You can buy them ready-made in packets or tins, though they are much nicer warm and fresh. *Crêpes dentelles* are paper-thin, lacy pancakes, a speciality of Quimper.

Cakes and Puddings

Like many Breton dishes, desserts tend to be very rich and heavy. One famous local cake is *far breton*, a solid flan containing prunes or raisins (▶ panel opposite). *Kouign-aman* is a delicious and fattening pastry of sugar, butter and almonds. *Galettes de Pont-Aven* (not to be confused with pancakes) are buttery biscuits like shortbread.

Drinks

Brittany produces little wine, apart from Loire-Atlantique's Muscadet (which now officially belongs to the Pays de la Loire region). The local tipples are cider (*cidre*) or barley beer (*cervoise*). Tastings are offered all over the region in cider museums or breweries. Stronger applejack potions are also on sale. *Pommeau* is a local apéritif. *Lambig* is the Breton equivalent of the Norman *calvados*, though quite hard to track down. Another local drink is *chouchen*, a honey-based mead. A sparkling variety is also made.

Buckwheat

The main ingredient of *galette* pancakes is not a cereal crop, but a sorrel-like plant with small white flowers. It originates in the Middle East, and its French name is sarrasin ('*saracen*') from its discovery during the Crusades. Most is now imported, though it can be grown in Brittany. You may find small display patches of it at local *écomusées*.

➕ 29D2
🍴 Good choice throughout resort (€–€€€)
🚌 Réseau Atlantic Lines 81 (Batz-sur-Mer–La Baule–St-Nazaire)
🚆 TGV Paris–Le Croisic
ℹ️ Place du 18 Juin 1940;
   ☎ 02 40 23 00 70
❓ Aug: craft market held in La Criée (fish market)

Océarium

✉️ Avenue de St-Goustan
☎ 02 40 23 02 44;
   www.ocearium-croisic.fr
🕐 Daily 10–12, 2–6 (Jul until 7). Closed Jan
🍴 On-site snack-bar (€)
♿ Good 💰 Expensive
❓ Fish fed by hand by a scuba diver

➕ 29D2
🍴 Good choice in old town, such as Roc Maria (€) ✉️ 1 rue du Vieux Marché aux Grains ☎ 02 40 24 90 51 (▶ 98)
🚌 A major regional route-hub: Réseau Atlantic Lines 80 (St-Nazaire), 83 (La Baule), 84 (Le Pouliguen), 85 (Mesquer), 86 (Asserac), 87 St-Lyphard
ℹ️ 1 place du Marché au Bois
   ☎ 02 40 24 96 71

Top: *Centre of Le Croisic*
Above: *Fortified gateway, Guérande*

LE CROISIC ⊙⊙

Le Croisic occupies a bulbous headland on the shores of the Grand Traict lagoon. Three islets linked by bridges form separate basins in the port, a picturesque scene when the fishing fleets arrive with catches of prawn. A modern *criée* (fish market) occupies one of these islands. Visitors may watch the early-morning proceedings from a gallery (5AM). The pleasantly shabby old town nearby contains 17th-century houses with wrought-iron balconies and dormer windows. Port-Lin, on the bracing ocean side of Le Croisic, is the main resort area, where several hotels overlook the waves crashing on dark rocks. Le Croisic's main attraction is its splendid **Océarium**, a star-shaped aquarium with well-organised displays of local and exotic species. The fish-farming exhibits are particularly interesting: baby eels and fingernail-sized turbot gulp gently at their spectators, and mussels cluster like maritime grapes on wooden posts (*bouchots*). The shark tank has a slightly alarming 'walk-through' tunnel.

GUÉRANDE ⊙⊙

The medieval ramparts encircling Guérande are visible for miles across the flat *marais salants* (saltmarshes). Inside these tower-studded walls, the old town is a maze of quaint streets with overhanging timber-framed houses. The Porte St-Michel (the former governor's residence) contains an idiosyncratic local history museum.

South of Guérande, heaps of salt fringe a mosaic of glittering pools linked by sluice gates and drainage channels. Egrets and herons patrol the pans for fish. Seawater floods into the larger lagoons at high tide, trickling gradually into ever-smaller and shallower clay-lined pits (*oeillets*) to evaporate in the sun and wind. Purified salt is on sale by the roadside. Visit the nearby **Maison des Paludiers** (saltworkers' house; tel: 02 40 62 21 96) or the **Terre de Sel**, a lively interactive discovery centre on the salt industry (www.seldeguerande.com).

LA GRANDE BRIÈRE ⬤⬤

Before the last Ice Age, the low-lying basin north of La Baule was covered with woodland. When the ice melted and sea levels rose, the area flooded and a thick layer of peat was formed. Gradually the sea retreated, and the marshes were drained and settled. The native Brierons developed an insular lifestyle based on hunting, fishing and turf cutting. Using local reeds to thatch their cottages and make wicker fish-traps, they negotiated the marshes in flat-bottomed punts.

In 1970, the Grande Brière was designated a 20,000ha regional nature park. It is now a popular holiday area offering fishing, riding, birdwatching and boating. The main villages of Kerhinet, St-Lyphard and St-Joachim are clusters of tidily restored thatched cottages; several house restaurants, craft-shops or little *ecomusées*. Le Musée du Chaume (Thatch Museum), La Maison de l'Eclusier (Lock-Keeper's House) and La Maison de la Mariée (the Bride's House) are examples. La Réserve Ornithologique is a nature reserve with walks and hides (binocular hire).

🔳 29E2

🍴 Several typical thatched *auberges* serve regional specialities, such as Auberge du Parc (€€)
✉ Ile de Fédrun
☎ 02 40 88 53 01

🚌 Réseau Atlantic Line 87 (Guérande–La Madeleine–St-Lyphard)

🚤 Barge or punt (*chaland* or *blain*) hire or trips through the marshes

🛈 38 rue de la Brière, La Chapelle-des-Marais
☎ 02 40 66 85 01;
www.parc-naturel-briere.fr

Left: *Reeds are still used for thatching in the Brière Regional National Park*

Below: *A traditional blin (flat-bottomed punt)*

NANTES ●●●

Nantes is a sophisticated regional capital with extensive industrial suburbs. Its historic centre is full of interest, with good shops, restaurants and museums, most of it compact enough to explore on foot. It makes a good base for visiting the vineyards and châteaux of the Loire Valley, and has lots of cultural activity and evening entertainment.

Brittany's beloved Duchess Anne was born in its mighty castle in 1477. In 1598, Henri IV signed the historic Edict of Nantes here, ending religious conflict for almost a century. During the 16th to 18th centuries Nantes prospered on the notorious 'ebony' (slave) trade with Africa and the Caribbean. As the Loire silted up, the port became inaccessible to large cargo vessels and Nantes diversified into other industries. Much of its attractive 18th- and 19th-century architecture remains intact despite war damage.

The Château des Ducs de Bretagne was built by François II (Duchess Anne's father) in 1466. It has been greatly altered throughout the centuries and is currently undergoing a massive restoration programme. When completed (2008), it will function as an integral part of an ambitious museum devoted to the history of Nantes. Only

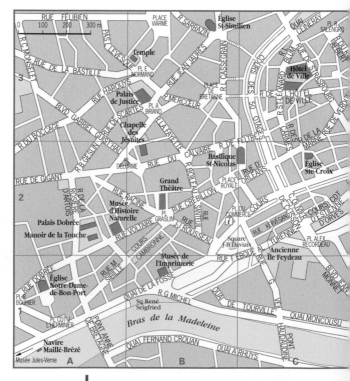

the courtyard and ramparts can be visited free of charge. The **Musée Jules-Verne** has the largest collection of manuscripts, portraits and objects once belonging to the writer born in Nantes in 1828. Near by in the upper town are the Cathédrale St-Pierre (➤ 26, Top Ten), and the **Musée des Beaux-Arts** (Fine Arts Museum), strong on 19th- and 20th-century art. The Jardin des Plantes, laid out in English style in 1865, contains an extensive collection of ancient magnolias and a huge Palmarium with a miniature jungle of exotic plants.

Towards the lower town, the 15th- and 16th-century houses of Ste-Croix and the shipowners' mansions in the Ancienne Ile Feydeau are full of detail. Art nouveau and neo-classical buildings stud the grand squares of place Royal and place Graslin. The **Palais Dobrée** was the former home of a wealthy Nantes shipowner. It contains an excellent archaeological collection and many eclectic *objets d'art*, including a casket which once held the heart of the Duchess Anne.The **Musée d'Histoire Naturelle** is a fascinating 19th-century collection. Its most bizarre exhibit is the skin of a soldier whose dying wish was to be made into a drum.

Musée Jules Verne
- ✉ 3 rue de l'Hermitage
- ☎ 02 40 69 72 52
- 🕐 Daily 10–12, 2–6. Closed Tue & Sun AM

Musée des Beaux-Arts
- ✉ 20 rue Clémenceau
- ☎ 02 40 41 65 65
- 🕐 Wed–Mon 10–6, Fri 10–8

Palais Dobrée
- ✉ 18 rue Voltaire
- ☎ 02 40 71 03 50
- 🕐 Tue–Fri 9:45–5:30, Sat–Sun 2:30–5:30

Musée d'Histoire Naturelle
- ✉ 12 rue Voltaire
- ☎ 02 40 99 26 20
- 🕐 Wed–Sun 10–6

Nantes' place Royal

Walk in the old town of Nantes

Distance
4km

Time
Allow most of the day if you want to see museums or do some shopping.

Start point
Place St-Pierre
✚ 77D3

End point
Palais Dobrée
✚ 76A2

Lunch
Brasserie La Cigale (€€)
✉ 4 place Graslin
☎ 02 51 84 94 94

Opposite: *St-Nazaire's small memorial park*

Below: *Exploring the quiet, narrow alleyways of Nantes*

Start in the place St–Pierre (by the cathedral).

After visiting the main sights (castle, cathedral and fine arts museum), relax for a while in the Jardin des Plantes.

Head back along rue de Richebourg, deviating briefly to the late Gothic Chapelle de l'Immaculée. Skirting the château, make for the Ste–Croix district via rue du Chât.

This is one of the oldest and most delightful parts of Nantes. Here 15th- and 16th-century houses line the streets (see rue de la Boucherie, rue de la Juiverie and rue Bossuet near the church of Ste-Croix).

Walk down rue d'Orléans to place Royale.

Here the architecture leaps ahead a couple of hundred years to the 18th century. The central fountain represents the Loire and its tributaries. A block southwest, passage Pommeraye is an elegant *fin-de-siècle* shopping centre.

Take rue de la Pérouse from place Royale, then turn west into place du Commerce (the tourist office is here).

The Ancienne Ile Feydeau to the southeast, once embraced by arms of the Loire, is no longer an island. It has many wealthy shipowners' houses decorated with quaint carvings and ornate wrought-ironwork.

Head up rue J J Rousseau into place Graslin.

This fine square has a mix of 18th- and 19th-century buildings, best appreciated from the tables outside the Brasserie La Cigale (➤ 98). The art nouveau interior is a riot of mirrors, mosaic tiles and swirling plasterwork.

Take Cours Cambronne southwest of place Graslin, another fine collection of 18th– and 19th–century houses. Head for the waterfront (quai de la Fosse).

The Musée de l'Imprimerie is an interesting little museum of printing, with working machinery.

Finish the walk at the Dobrée museum complex (➤ 77) on rue Voltaire.

ST-NAZAIRE ✪

This unfortunate place was all but obliterated during World War II, though ironically, the main focus of the attacks (the concrete submarine pens housing German U-boats) survived more or less intact. The rest of the city, pulverised by the Allies, was rebuilt after the war in rather brutal, functional concrete. Today, several of its high-profile visitor attractions in the restored docklands area reveal St-Nazaire's key role in France's long maritime history.

The **Ecomusée** at the heart of the port traces the story of the town, with special emphasis on the wartime era. The best section is the submarine exit, a covered lock from which U-boats could slip out of the harbour in secret. It now contains the French nuclear-powered submarine, *Espadon*, which once sailed the polar ice-caps (the museum ticket includes a tour of the vessel – living quarters, engines and torpedo room). There's a fine view of the estuary and the port from the blockhouse terrace.

St-Nazaire's once-flourishing shipbuilding industry is now in serious decline, but a few vessels are still constructed here. **Escal'Atlantic** is an impressive discovery centre re-creating the world of the ocean liner, with multi-media special effects and historic movie footage. Other attractions in the port complex include the **Chantiers de l'Atlantique** (a working shipyard) and **Aérospatiale**, where the French Airbus is assembled, (reservations necessary for both; you will need your passport).

South of the town a graceful suspension bridge arcs across the Loire, measuring a span of 3,556m, providing a fast link from Brittany to the Atlantic seaboard.

✚ 29E2

🍴 Plenty of choice in centre; nearer port is Le Grand Café (€) ✉ Place des 4 Z'Horloges ☎ 02 40 22 37 66

🚍 Réseau Atlantic route-hub: Lines 80 (Guérande), 81 (La Baule), 82 (Pornichet), 83 (St-Marc)

ℹ Boulevard de la Légion d'Honneur ☎ 02 40 22 40 65

Port museums and dockland attractions

✉ Ville-Port

☎ 0 810 888 444

🕐 JEscal'Atlantic & *Espadon*: Jul–Aug daily 9:30–7:30; Apr–Jun, Sep–Oct daily 9:30–12:30, 1:30–6; Feb–Mar, Nov–Dec Wed–Sun 10–12:30, 2–6. Closed Jan

♿ Few (none at the *Espadon*)

🎟 Expensive (combined tickets available)

DID YOU KNOW?

St-Marc, southwest of St-Nazaire, is a place of pilgrimage for cinema fans. Jacques Tati's classic *Monsieur Hulot's Holiday* (1953) was filmed here at the Hôtel de la Plage. The French are still puzzled by the film's enormous popularity among English speakers.

Morbihan

The name Morbihan means 'Little Sea' in Breton, a reference to the *département's* most striking geographical feature. The Golfe du Morbihan, a huge tidal lagoon, is a strange, landlocked maze of muddy creeks and grass-topped islands. In summer it buzzes with excursion boats and flurrying sails. It's an important over-wintering ground for countless migrant seabirds and wildfowl.

Morbihan's megaliths are world-famous. Carnac's *alignements* (mysterious lines of standing stones) is one of the region's prime visitor attractions, rivalled by Locmariaquer and the island of Gavrinis, which boasts Brittany's most ornate prehistoric tomb.

The low-lying coastline lacks the drama of the Pink Granite or Emerald coasts, but sheltered sandy beaches and offshore islands, especially Belle-Ile, compensate. Exploring the area via the Nantes–Brest Canal offers a new dimension.

> '*The boats were crammed in, gunwale to gunwale...Oh, the wonderful confusion of mooring ropes, which crossed over each other, got tangled up in tillers and grappling-hooks, and plunged beneath the keels.* '

HENRI QUEFFELEC,
Six Sailors of Groix, describing Morbihan's
tuna-fishing industry during the 1930s

Aerial view over Morbihan

What to See in Morbihan
AURAY ⭐⭐

This ancient place has played a significant role in Breton history, and is designated one of the region's nine *villes d'art et d'histoire*. It is now a bustling and sizeable town, and its principal activities include tourism and oyster-raising. Auray is believed to be the last place reached by Julius Caesar in his conquest of Gaul. The Romans established their camp in the river port known today as St-Goustan and now the most picturesque part of the town. Flower-decked, timbered houses and inns surround the quayside place St-Sauveur and the hilly streets near by. Benjamin Franklin, forced ashore by a storm, once spent a night here in 1776 while drumming up French support for the American War of Independence. The eye-catching schooner moored by the quayside is an old tuna-fishing vessel. It contains a small **museum** of local maritime history. Across a quaint 17th-century stone bridge, the church of St-Gildas in the town centre has a fine Renaissance porch and a marble altarpiece dating from 1664.

On Auray's northwestern outskirts, shrines and chapels commemorate the martyred members of the Chouan movement led by Georges Cadoudal, who staged an unsuccessful Royalist uprising against Revolutionary forces in 1795. To the northeast of Auray, Ste-Anne-d'Auray is one of Brittany's most important religious sites. A colourful *pardon* on 25 and 26 July (the Feast of St Anne) attracts

---

➕ 29D3

🍴 Cafés, *crêperies* and restaurants in the old town and port (€–€€)

🚌 Réseau TIM Lines 16 (Etel), 01 (Quiberon–Vannes), 05 (Baud), 06 (Golfe du Morbihan–Vannes)

🚉 SNCF rail connections to Vannes, Quiberon and Lorient

🚢 Pleasure cruises on the River Auray or to the Golfe du Morbihan

ℹ️ 20 rue du Lait ☎ 02 97 24 09 75 (Auray) ✉ 12 place Nicolazic ☎ 02 97 57 69 16 (Ste-Anne-d'Auray)

❓ 25 & 26 Jul: *Pardon* of Ste-Anne (Ste-Anne-d'Auray)

Musée de Goëlette

✉ Port de St-Goustan
☎ 02 97 56 63 38
🕐 Apr–Sep daily 10–7
♿ None 💷 Cheap

82

Fishing boats in the sleepy little town of Auray

thousands of pilgrims to its gloomy basilica, built in honour of a 17th-century ploughman's miraculous vision. Of more general interest is the vast war memorial alongside, dedicated to the 250,000 Bretons who perished in the Great War.

BELLE-ILE-EN-MER ✪✪

Brittany's largest island is also one of its most attractive, as its name suggests. Just 14km offshore, it makes an immensely popular excursion from the ferry-port of Quiberon, near Carnac. Attractive beaches and varied scenery, historic sights and good holiday facilities are the main reasons to venture here. Most people go just for a day-trip and explore the island on a guided coach tour, but Belle-Ile's appealing hotels make longer stays feasible (book well ahead; they are often over-subscribed in high season).

Ferry passengers land at Le Palais, Belle-Ile's capital. Above the harbour, packed with shops, cafés and hotels, looms the star-shaped **Citadel**, built during the 16th century by Vauban (Louis XIV's military architect). A former prison and garrison, it now houses a museum of local history. In 1763, Belle-Ile was an English possession. It was exchanged for Menorca at the Treaty of Paris.

Belle-Ile is divided into four parishes named after the main villages. The interior consists of a plateau of moorland schist cut by fertile sheltered valleys that protect the white houses from the prevailing wind. The east coast has good safe beaches with watersports facilities; Grandes Sables is the largest and best. The west coast is ruggedly beautiful but dangerous, with a fiordlike inlet at Port-Goulphar. Monet is alleged to have painted the photogenically gnawed rock stacks (Les Aiguilles – the Pinnacles) at Port-Coton no less than 38 times. Sauzon, on the northeast side, is a charming, photogenic little lobster-fishing port with colourwashed cottages and a lighthouse. A fort on the nearby Pointe des Poulains was once the holiday home of the celebrated actress Sarah Bernhardt. It was destroyed by the Germans in World War II.

28C2

🍴 Cafés and restaurants in the main centres, such as Café Atlantique (€–€€)
☎ Quai de l'Arcadie, Le Palais

🚌 Taol Mor Line 21 (Le Palais–Sauzon); excursion buses tour the island

🚢 Dozens of boat trips to and from Morbihan's main ports (mainly Quiberon)

ℹ Quai Bonelle, Le Palais
☎ 02 97 31 81 93

Citadel

✉ Le Palais
☎ 02 97 31 84 17
🕐 Daily 9:30–6 (7 in high season); Nov–Mar 9:30–noon, 2–5
♿ None
💷 Moderate

Sunset over Morbihan

➕ 29D2

Cairn de Gavrinis
✉ Cale de Pen-Lannic, Ile de Gavrinis
☎ 02 97 57 19 38
🕐 Apr–Oct daily for guided tours (numbers limited, so book ahead)
♿ None
🚢 Boat trips and entrance tickets from Larmor Baden ☎ 02 97 57 19 38
💷 Expensive (includes ferry fare)

Château de Suscinio
✉ Kermoizan, Sarzeau
☎ 02 97 41 91 91
🕐 Apr–Sep daily 10–7; Feb–Mar, Oct–Nov Wed–Mon 10–12, 2–6; Dec–Jan Thu–Tue 10–12, 2–6
♿ None
💷 Moderate

CARNAC (➤ 16, TOP TEN)

GOLFE DU MORBIHAN ⭐⭐

The 'Little Sea' that forms such a prominent feature of the Morbihan coastline resulted from a fall in land levels several thousand years ago. It measures over 20km wide and 15km from north to south, a huge, almost landlocked lagoon. Vast numbers of migrant seabirds and wildfowl colonise its varied habitats, comprising dunes, mudflats, oyster beds, saltmarshes, creeks, reedbeds, heath and pine wood. Tender plants thrive in its sheltered micro-climate.

The muddy shores do not boast good beaches, and swimming can be dangerous; tides tear in and out of the narrow straits near Locmariaquer with great force. None the less, it is a popular holiday area, with hotels, restaurants and campsites sprinkled all around the shoreline. The small resorts along its wooded northern shores (such as Arradon and Baden) are particularly attractive. The main attraction is boating; in summer a mass of pleasure craft weaves among a host of hundreds of grassy islets. Several of these are accessible.

The lushly vegetated Ile aux Moines has pretty villas (sailings from Port-Blanc). The wilder, bleaker Ile d'Arz is linked by ferry from Conleau (the port of Vannes). If you have time to see only one, make it the Ile de Gavrinis, site of an elaborately carved **burial chamber** beneath a stone cairn.

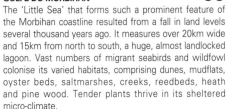

The long Presqu'ile de Rhuys (Rhuys peninsula) enclosing the gulf on the southern side has an exceptionally mild climate where camellias and figs flourish. The **Château de Suscinio** is the main sight, a lonely marshland fortress, now restored as a museum.

DID YOU KNOW?

The star-crossed 12th-century lovers Abelard and Héloïse are associated with the Rhuys peninsula. After their affair was discovered, Abelard was forced into exile as abbot of St-Gildas-de-Rhuys – 'a wild country where every day brings new perils', he wrote. All too true; his fellow monks tried to poison him but he managed to escape down a secret passage.

Left: *Josselin's mighty castle has elaborate granite carvings overlooking its courtyard*

Below: *Locmariaquer's huge menhir weighs 35 tonnes*

JOSSELIN ✪✪

The most memorable feature of this enticing medieval town is its mighty fortress, mirrored in the clear waters of the Oust. The turreted **Château** dates mainly from the 14th century, when the town passed into the hands of the Rohan family. Its Renaissance façade was added around the turn of the 16th century. The charming **Musée des Poupées** (doll museum) in the stable-block contains exhibits several centuries old.

In the town centre, the 12th-century church of Notre-Dame-du-Roncier (Our Lady of the Brambles), contains the tomb of Josselin's erstwhile master, Olivier de Clisson, Constable of France. A *pardon* reveres the patron Virgin. Northeast of Josselin, the Forêt de Paimpont is a popular touring and walking area, mainly for its Arthurian legends. Ploërmel, en route, was the site of a famous chivalric tournament in 1351, known as the Battle of the Thirty.

LOCMARIAQUER ✪✪

This pretty oyster port guarding the neck of the Golfe du Morbihan rivals Carnac in archaeological importance. Its main sights lie in a fenced compound north of the village. They include a huge recumbent menhir, broken into four sections. If it ever stood upright it would have measured over 20m high. Near by is a large decorated dolmen, the **Table des Marchands,** one of several good examples to be seen in the area. In Roman times the town of *Dariorigum* stood on this site, and the Gaullish *Veneti* used it as their naval base. Today, Locmariaquer is a peaceful place with attractive south-facing beaches, a pleasant old harbour quarter and lots of boat trips. Seafront walks and views from the Pointe de Kerpenhir are excellent.

➕ 29D3
🍴 Cafés and restaurants in old town (€–€€)
🚌 Réseau TIM Line 81 (Pontivy–Ploërmel)
ℹ Place de la Congrégation ☎ 02 97 22 36 43

Château de Josselin/ Musée des Poupées
☎ 02 97 22 36 45
🕐 Jul–Aug daily 10–6; Jun & Sep daily 2–6; Apr–May Wed, Sat–Sun & hols 2–6
♿ Good
💶 Moderate (combined ticket available)

➕ 29D2
🍴 Attractive hotel-restaurants by port, such as L'Escale or Lautram (€€)
ℹ Rue de la Victoire ☎ 02 97 57 33 05; www.golfe-du-morbihan.com
🚢 Boat trips round Golfe du Morbihan; crossings to Belle-Ile and Port-Navalo

Site Megalithique de la Table des Marchands
✉ Rute de Kerlogonan
☎ 02 97 57 37 59
🕐 May–Sep 10–7; Oct–Apr 10–12:30, 2–5
♿ Good
💶 Moderate (combined ticket available for Carnac museum)

28C3

A few modest options in town centre (€–€€)

TIM Line 18 (Carnac)

La Mairie
☎ 02 97 82 52 93

Musée de la Marine/Musée de la Compagnie des Indes

✉ Citadelle de Port-Louis

☎ Musée Marine 02 97 82 56 72, Musée Compagnie des Indes 02 97 82 19 13; www.lorient.com/musee

🕐 Apr–mid-Sep daily 10–6:30; mid-Sep–Mar Wed–Mon 2–6. Closed mid-Dec–Feb

♿ Good

💰 Moderate

28C2

Good choice of bars and restaurants by the port (€–€€)

TIM Line 01 (Auray–Plouharnel)

SNCF connections (Auray–Vannes)

Frequent ferries to Belle-Ile; also to Houat and Hoëdic islands

14 rue de Verdun
☎ 02 97 50 07 84

PORT-LOUIS ⭐⭐

Port-Louis was named after Louis XIV, under whose reign the town flourished. It became the first headquarters of the Compagnie des Indes (East India Company) set up by Cardinal Richelieu. The venture failed and in 1666 the operation was transferred across the water to Lorient. Port-Louis avoided the devastating air-raids of World War II that destroyed much of Lorient, and retains the air of a modest fishing port.

The fortified citadel at the harbour entrance was founded in 1591, and later used as a prison, barracks and arsenal. It now houses an enjoyable museum complex which includes the **Musée de la Marine** (maritime museum) and the **Musée de la Compagnie des Indes**, dedicated to the history of the East India Company during the 17th and 18th centuries. Rampart walks give excellent views of the Lorient roadsteads.

East of Port-Louis, the Etel estuary offers quiet picnic spots among an intricate maze of sandbanks, islands and oysterbeds. The village of St-Cado is much visited.

PRESQU'ILE DE QUIBERON ⭐⭐

A narrow neck of tidal sediment links this feather-shaped peninsula with the mainland, in places barely wider than the access road which runs past windswept conifers and dunes of blown sand. The resort of Quiberon is one of Morbihan's liveliest. Besides its attractions of good sandy beaches and a thalassotherapy centre, it is the main ferry terminal for Belle-Ile and always crowded in summer.

Quiberon has a sailing school based in its sheltered eastern waters. The west coast is the Côte Sauvage, where the Atlantic beats furiously on cliffs, crags and caves. The Pointe de Percho offers good views.

La Roche-Bernard's elegant suspension bridge spans the River Vilaine

LA ROCHE-BERNARD ✪✪

Since the building of the Arzal dam, the Vilaine no longer provides an outlet to the open sea, and pleasure craft are the only boats to reach the town. In years gone by, however, La Roche-Bernard was a great riverine trading centre, handling cargoes of grain, wine, salt and timber. The **Musée de la Vilaine Maritime**, housed in the Château des Basses-Fosses on the west bank of the river, recounts these prosperous times (tel: 02 99 90 83 47). Today, the town's revenue comes mainly from tourism. Classed as a *petite cité de charactère*, it makes a most attractive touring base, with an excellent range of restaurants and hotels. The old quarter is packed with charming, flower-decked houses. A graceful suspension bridge spans the river, replacing an earlier version accidentally destroyed when lightning struck a German ammunition base.

🔲	29E2
🍴	Several outstanding, if expensive restaurants-with-rooms (€€–€€€), such as Auberge Bretonne 🔲 Place Duguesclin (€€€) ☎ 02 99 90 60 28
🚌	Réseau TIM Line 08 (Vannes–Nantes)
🚢	Boat trips on the Vilaine to Redon and the Arzal dam
ℹ️	14 rue Dr-Cornudet ☎ 02 99 90 67 98

ROCHEFORT-EN-TERRE ✪✪

The attractions of this village are immediately obvious. The setting on a schist spur surrounded by plunging wooded slopes and rushing water is a postcard scene. Patrician mansions decorated with carvings and window-boxes line a cobbled street restored to tastefully pristine condition. Rochefort's main source of revenue is tourism, yet it retains its dignity and a sense of life with classy shops and restaurants. The 12th-century church of Notre-Dame-de-la-Tronchaye was granted collegiate status in 1498. Points of interest include a 16th-century calvary, a fine gallery and Renaissance altarpieces. The **castle** at the top of the town was restored at the beginning of the 20th century, and contains a small museum.

🔲	29D3
🍴	Attractive choices in old town
🚌	TIM Lines 09 (Vannes), 10 (Redon)
ℹ️	Place des Halles ☎ 02 97 43 33 57; www.golfe-du-morbihan.com

Château et Musée de Rochefort-en-Terre

☎ 02 97 43 31 56
⏰ Apr–May Sat–Sun 2–6:30; Jun, Sep daily 2–6:30; Jul–Aug daily 10–6:30. Closed Oct–Mar
♿ None
🖐 Moderate

The small village of Rochefort-en-Terre is a gem of domestic architecture

<table>
<tbody>
<tr><td>✚</td><td>29D2</td></tr>
<tr><td>🍴</td><td>Good choice of bars, cafés and restaurants in the old town (€–€€€)</td></tr>
<tr><td>🚌</td><td>Regional route-hub: TIM Lines 01 (Auray), 02 (Baud), 03 (Pontivy), 04 (Ploërmel), 05 (Ste-Anne-d'Auray), 06 (Arradon/Golfe du Morbihan), 07 (Rhuys peninsula), 08 (La Roche-Bernard), 09 (Rochefort-en-Terre)</td></tr>
<tr><td>🚆</td><td>SNCF connections with Redon/Nantes, Auray/Quiberon and Lorient. TGV line Paris–Quimper</td></tr>
<tr><td>🚢</td><td>Wide range around Golfe du Morbihan, and to Belle-Ile</td></tr>
<tr><td>ℹ️</td><td>1 rue Thiers ☎ 02 97 47 24 34</td></tr>
<tr><td>❓</td><td>A petit train provides tours of the old town (with commentary)</td></tr>
</tbody>
</table>

La Cohue/Musée des Beaux-Arts

- ✉ 9 & 15 place St-Pierre
- ☎ 02 97 47 35 86
- 🕐 Mid-Jun–Sep daily 10–6; off-peak 1:30–6 (closed Sun & hols)
- ♿ Good
- 💶 Moderate (charges vary for temporary exhibitions)

Capitaine d'un Jour

- ✉ Parc du Golfe
- ☎ 02 97 40 40 39
- 🕐 Daily 9:30–7. Closed Jan
- ♿ Good
- 💶 Moderate

VANNES ✪✪✪

This busy commercial city has a long, prestigious history. When the Romans arrived, Vannes was the capital of the *Veneti*, the Armorican tribe defeated by Caesar in 56 BC. In the 9th century it resumed its leading role under Nominoë, first Duke of Brittany, and shared its primacy with Nantes until union with France in 1532. Today it is one of Brittany's best-looking towns, more cosmopolitan than most.

Its well-preserved old quarter lies behind imposing ramparts, best observed from the promenade de la Garenne, a raised walkway beside colourful public gardens. Vannes' most picturesque sight, the old *lavoir* (washhouse), stands near the Porte Poterne. The main monument within the walls is the Cathédrale St-Pierre, a hotchpotch of styles from Romanesque to baroque. The tomb of Vannes' patron, St Vincent Ferrier, a saint of Spanish origin, lies in the Rotunda Chapel. The cathedral also houses the wizened finger of the Blessed Pierre Rogue, guillotined at Vannes in 1796. Opposite the cathedral, **La Cohue** is a medieval covered market that once housed the lawcourts. This building now provides display space for temporary exhibitions and the **Musée des Beaux-Arts**, containing an assortment of Breton paintings. Its star exhibit is Eugène Delacroix's *Crucifixion*.

A wander through Old Vannes reveals many other handsome buildings and squares. The place des Lices, once used for medieval tournaments, holds a produce market every Wednesday and Saturday. Near by are the Maison de Vannes, adorned with quaint carvings of a rustic couple popularly known as Vannes and his Wife, and the Maison de St-Vincent Ferrier.

Vannes is one of southern Brittany's main excursion centres, principally offering boat trips on the Golfe du Morbihan. Pleasure craft moor outside the walled old town, at the *gare maritime* on the Conleau peninsula. The Parc du Golfe here is a leisure park with a huge saltwater swimming pool and several other family attractions, including a **butterfly garden**, **aquarium** and the **Capitaine d'un Jour**, where you can embark on a trip through the

Le Jardin aux Papillons (butterfly garden)
- ⊠ Parc du Golfe
- ☎ 02 97 46 01 02
- ⏰ Jun–Aug daily 10–6; Apr–May, Sep daily 10–12:30, 2–5:30
- ♿ Good
- 👆 Moderate

Aquarium de Vannes
- ⊠ Parc du Golfe
- ☎ 02 97 40 67 40
- ⏰ Apr–May, Sep 9–12, 1:30–7; Jun–Aug 9–8; Oct–Mar 10–12:30, 1:30–6:30
- ♿ Good
- 👆 Moderate

Medieval washhouses in Vannes

ages, navigate through the currents of the Golfe de Morbihan, or become 'a ship's captain for a day'.

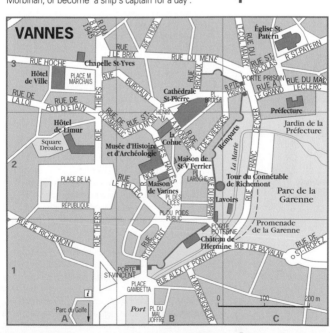

Walk through the Old Town of Vannes

Distance
3km

Time
Allow half a day with time for sightseeing

Start point
Tourist office (rue Thiers)
✚ 89A1

End point
Place Gambetta
✚ 89B1

Lunch
La Table au Gourmet (€€)
✉ 6 rue A Le Pontois
☎ 02 97 47 52 44 (rampart views)

Start from the tourist office in rue Thiers and head northeast to place Gambetta, just north of the canalised port.

Place Gambetta consists of a terraced crescent of 19th-century buildings, especially lively with cafés and bars in the early evening.

Enter the ramparts via the Porte St-Vincent, and proceed up rue St-Vincent to the place des Lices.

The largely pedestrianised streets inside the walls are a relief after the noisy traffic outside. Place des Lices, once a medieval tiltyard, is now the marketplace. Just north of the square, on the corner of rue Noë, stands the quaint Maison de Vannes. Near by is Vannes' history and archaeology museum, in an elegant urban manor called the Château Gaillard. It contains a fine collection of prehistoric objects.

Head northeast to the place Valencia.

At No 17 stands the home of St Vincent Ferrier, the town's patron saint, marked by a niched statue.

Head up rue des Orfevres, and visit the Cathédrale St-Pierre and La Cohue. Then stroll west from place Henri IV along rue St-Salomon to rue Thiers.

Here are the imposing Hôtel de Limur (a 17th-century town house), and (on place M Marchais) the 19th-century Hôtel de Ville with its fine equestrian statue.

Walk back past the cathedral via rue Burgault and rue des Chanoines. Pass through the machicolated Porte-Prison, then head south past the ramparts along the promenade de la Garenne.

Fine 16th-century gabled and half-timbered houses in the centre of Vannes

Bright waterside gardens cheer up the stern rampart towers. Notice the picturesque 18th-century *lavoir* (washhouse) by the bridge near Porte Poterne.

Return to place Gambetta and the port, near the starting point.

Where To...

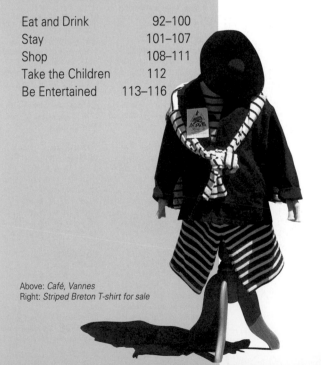

Above: *Café, Vannes*
Right: *Striped Breton T-shirt for sale*

Finistère

Prices
Prices are based on a three-course meal for one, without wine:

€ = up to €20
€€ = €20–50
€€€ = over €50

Unless otherwise specified, assume places stay open for lunch and dinner, or throughout the day. Many of the hotels listed in Where to Stay (▶ 101–107) also have good restaurants.

Bénodet

L'Agape (€€€)
A lovely old house quietly set some way behind the resort. The ambience is elegant and refined, with expensive, carefully presented menus.
✉ Route de la Plage ☎ 02 98 56 32 70 🕐 Closed Jan–Feb, Sun eve (except Jul–Aug), Tue lunch, Mon

La Cabane du Pêcheur (€)
Cheerful seafront *crêperie* with nautical décor near the casino. Excellent pancakes filled with a variety of interesting regional produce. Children's menus; pizzas, omelettes etc.
✉ 37 rond point du Poulquer ☎ 02 98 66 27 97 🕐 Closed Nov, Mon, Tue (except school hols)

Brest

Maison de l'Océan (€€)
A terrific choice of seafood in this lively restaurant down by the docks. Not far from the Château and central museums. Tables outside.
✉ 2 quai Douane ☎ 02 98 80 44 84 🕐 Lunch, dinner

Ma Petite Folie (€€)
This former lobster boat is moored in the pleasure port and serves delicious fishy fare like grilled lobster and potted crab. Lots of daily specials.
✉ Port de Plaisance ☎ 02 98 42 44 42 🕐 Closed 1–10 Jan

Concarneau

Chez Armande (€€)
Unpretentious, family-run fish restaurant serving excellent menus at good prices.
✉ 15 bis avenue Dr Nicolas ☎ 02 98 97 00 76 🕐 Closed Christmas, mid-Feb–early Mar, Wed, Tue off-season

Le Conquet

Relais de Vieux Port (€)
A charming, breezily decorated little dining room by the harbour serving simple snacks, *crêpes*, salads etc. Live music Wednesday evenings in summer. Stylish rooms available.
✉ 1 quai Drellach ☎ 02 98 89 15 91 🕐 Closed Jan

Crozon

Hostellerie de la Mer (€€)
Terraces and picture windows make the most of the glorious sea views in this pretty hotel-restaurant specialising in fish dishes.
✉ Le Fret ☎ 02 98 27 61 90 🕐 Lunch, dinner

Mutin Gourmand (€€)
Acclaimed for its skilful seafood cooking, you'll find whatever's best and freshest from the market at this charmingly decorated hotel-restaurant, including some unusual creatures.
✉ Place de l'Eglise ☎ 02 98 27 06 51 🕐 Closed Sun eve, Mon, Tue lunch

Guimiliau

Ar Chupen (€)
A short walk from the church, this restaurant is in a renovated Breton farmhouse. A wide choice of fillings for their lacy galettes.
✉ 43 rue du Guililiau ☎ 02 98 68 73 63 🕐 Lunch, dinner

Locronan

Ty Coz (€)
Charming flower-decked *crêperie* and *glacier* in an old stone building on the main square.
✉ Place de l'Eglise ☎ 02 98 81 70 79 🕐 Closed Oct–Easter, Mon (except school hols)

Morlaix
Marée Bleue (€€)
Traditional menus and interesting wines in an elegant, cosy restaurant in an alley just off Morlaix's main square.

✉ 3 rampe St-Mélaine ☎ 02 98 63 24 21 ⏰ Closed Oct, Sun eve, Mon

Plogoff
Hôtel de la Baie des Trépassés (€€)
Good-value seafood menus in a spectacular coastal location on Cap Sizun. Can get very busy.

✉ Pointe du Raz ☎ 02 98 70 61 34 ⏰ Closed mid-Nov to mid-Feb

Plougonvelin
Hostellerie de la Pointe St-Mathieu (€€)
Elaborate seafood dishes in the vaulted stone restaurant of an attractively modernised hotel set on a headland.

✉ Pointe St-Mathieu ☎ 02 98 89 00 19 ⏰ Closed Sun eve off-season

Pont-Aven
Café des Arts (€)
Popular, lively *brasserie* with live music, good beer and simple, well-prepared dishes such as Mexican *fajitas*.

✉ 11 rue du Général du Gaulle ☎ 02 98 06 07 12 ⏰ Closed Thu off-season

Moulin de Rosmadec (€€€)
A picturesque restaurant with rooms set mid-stream in one of Pont-Aven's famous old watermills. Acclaimed cooking in memorably elegant surroundings.

✉ Venelle de Rosmadec ☎ 02 98 06 00 22 ⏰ Closed mid–end Oct, Feb hols, Wed, Sun eve off-season

Quimper
Crêperie du Sallé (€)
A delightful half-timbered building in the heart of the old town makes a fine setting for this friendly place. Outdoor tables on the square.

✉ 6 rue du Sallé ☎ 02 98 95 95 80 ⏰ Closed Sun, Mon

La Fleur de Sel (€€)
This place across the river from Quimper's *faïencerie* factories in Locmaria is a good bet for lunch. Great views and light fish dishes.

✉ 1 quai Neuf ☎ 02 98 55 04 71 ⏰ Closed early May, Christmas & New Year, Sat, Sun

Riec-sur-Bélon
Chez Jacky (€€)
Celebrated oyster farm and restaurant overlooking the River Bélon. An interesting place to try or buy oysters.

✉ Port de Bélon ☎ 02 98 06 90 32 ⏰ Closed Nov–Easter, Mon

Roscoff
Le Temps de Vivre (€€€)
Top-notch cooking at an old corsaire's house opposite the church. Lobster, onion and artichoke dishes are among its specialities.

✉ Place de l'Eglise ☎ 02 98 61 27 28 ⏰ Closed Oct, Mon, Tue lunch, Sun eve off-season

St Pol de Leon
Auberge la Pomme d'Api (€€)
This charming village centre restaurant offers succulent seafood dishes. Specialities include a dish of warm oysters, and fresh figs poached in sweet white wine.

✉ 49 rue Verderel ☎ 02 98 69 04 36 ⏰ Closed Sun, Tue eve, Mon

St-Thégonnec
Auberge St-Thégonnec (€€)
Superb cooking in a smart hotel-restaurant, an ideal base for exploring the parish closes.

✉ 6 place de la Mairie ☎ 02 98 79 61 18 ⏰ Closed late Dec–mid-Jan, Sat lunch, Sun eve, Mon off-season

Menu or Carte?
These terms are often confused by English-speaking visitors, because the French word for the menu (ie a printed list of what's cooking) is *la carte*. But in a French restaurant, a *menu*, meaning a *menu du jour* or *menu à prix fixe*, is a set-price, multi-course meal, often much cheaper than eating *à la carte* dishes ordered separately. Lunch *menus* are especially good value, sometimes quite affordable even in very grand establishments. There are usually several choices at each course, and drinks may be included if specified (*boisson/vin compris*). A *formule* is a simple *menu* which allows you to vary the number of courses you order. The dish of the day (*plat du jour*) is generally a safe bet.

Côtes d'Armor

Organic Produce

In Brittany, as elsewhere, consumer demand has led to an increasing concern with animal welfare and healthy eating. Farmers are returning to natural fertilisers like manure, compost and seaweed instead of artificial chemicals, and using traditional methods of crop rotation. Organic producers market their wares at fairs like 'Biozone' (held annually in September at Mûr-de-Bretagne). Chemical-free meat is awarded special certification such as the *Label Rouge* or *porc fermier de Bretagne* (free-range). Look out for the accreditation 'AB' or the word '*biologique*' in shops and restaurants, indicating produce has been grown organically.

Cap Fréhel

La Fauconnière (€)

Panoramic location by a dramatic Emerald Coast headland. Popular with walkers and bird-watchers for simple fare (omelettes, fresh fish, etc).

✉ À la Pointe ☎ 02 96 41 54 20 🕐 Closed Oct–mid-Mar, Wed

Dinan

Le Cantorbery (€€)

A popular place in one of Dinan's characterful half-timbered houses. Specialities include *pré-salé* lamb and potted fish.

✉ 6 rue Ste-Claire ☎ 02 96 39 02 52 🕐 Closed mid–end Nov, early Feb, Wed

Mère Pourcel (€€–€€€)

This quaint, 15th-century timbered building with its magnificent oak staircase is a well-known landmark in the heart of the old town. Accomplished cooking and generous helpings. Tables on the pedestrianised cobbles outside.

✉ 3 place des Merciers ☎ 02 96 39 03 80 🕐 Closed Feb, Mon, Tue in winter, Sun eve off-season

Le Romarin (€)

This welcoming *salon-de-thé* run by a mother-and-daughter team specialises in wonderful home-made cakes and sweet and savoury tarts and pies. Excellent house wine. Take-away service.

✉ 11 place des Cordeliers ☎ 02 96 85 20 37 🕐 10–5 only in winter (also Aug pm)

Erquy

L'Escurial (€€)

This plain but highly regarded restaurant near the harbour knows how to cook the town's famous scallops to perfection.

✉ Boulevard de la Mer ☎ 02 96 72 31 56 🕐 Closed late Jun, late Nov–early Jan, Mon, Sun eve off-season

Ile de Bréhat

Bellevue (€€)

Fresh seafood is the main component of the menus in this informal little hotel-restaurant near the quayside.

✉ Port Clos ☎ 02 96 20 00 05 🕐 Closed mid-Nov to mid-Dec, early Jan–early Feb

Lamballe

La Téte Noire (€)

Quaint old inn off the main square near dating from the 15th century. Also has an attractive, atmospheric bistro.

✉ 8 rue du Four ☎ 02 96 50 88 74 🕐 Closed Sun off-season

Mûr-de-Bretagne

Auberge Grand'Maison (€€€)

This smart restaurant-with-rooms in an inland lake resort deserves a pilgrimage for a special gastronomic treat. The *chef-patron* is one of the most respected chefs in Brittany. Reservation recommended.

✉ 1 rue Léon-le-Cerf ☎ 02 96 28 51 10 🕐 Closed early Mar, most of Oct, Sun eve, Mon, Tue off-season

Paimpol

Morel (€)

Very popular *crêperie* on the central marketplace, serving inventive fillings concocted from local produce accompanied by Breton cider.

✉ 11 place du Martray ☎ 02 96 20 86 34 🕐 Closed 2 weeks in Feb, 3 weeks in Nov, Sun off-season

La Vieille Tour (€€)

Good-value regional cooking is served in this modest stone-built house with an intimate dining room.

✉ 13 rue de l'Eglise ☎ 02 96 20 83 18 🕐 Closed Mon lunch Jul–Aug, Sun eve, Wed off-season

Perros-Guirec
Crêperie Hamon (€)

A well-known local secret, popular for its rustic setting and skilful pancake-tossing. Book ahead.

✉ 36 rue de la Salle ☎ 02 96 23 28 82 🕐 Closed Mon, Sun (except school hols)

Les Feux des Iles (€€)

Up-market hotel-restaurant with panoramic views towards Les Sopt-Iles from the dining room.

✉ 53 boulevard Clemenceau ☎ 02 96 23 22 94 🕐 Closed early Mar, early Oct, mid-Dec, Mon & Sun eve Oct–Apr

Plancoët
Jean-Pierre Crouzil (€€€)

Formidable cooking and a spectacular wine list at this celebrated restaurant-with-rooms some way inland. Stylish décor. Lobster, scallop and turbot specialities.

✉ 20 les Quais ☎ 02 96 84 10 24 🕐 Closed early Oct, mid-Jan, Mon; Sun eve, Tue lunch off-season

Pléneuf-Val-André
Au Biniou (€€)

A well-known local favourite for interestingly prepared seafood dishes in traditional, refined surroundings near the casino and Le Val-André's gleaming beach.

✉ 121 rue Clemenceau ☎ 02 96 72 24 35 🕐 Closed Feb, Tue eve, Wed off-season

Ploubalay
Restaurant de la Gare (€€)

The chef here uses only the freshest ingredients for the delicious fish dishes. Hold back a little and leave room for the dessert.

✉ 4 rue Ormelets Ploubalay ☎ 02 96 27 25 16 🕐 Closed Mon & Tue eve, Wed

Sables-d'Or-les-Pins
Voile d'Or (€€€)

This elegant hotel-restaurant has a notable seafood restaurant. Panoramic views over the tranquil expanses of an exceptionally pretty lagoon add to its attractions.

✉ Allée des Acacias ☎ 02 96 41 42 49 🕐 Closed mid-Nov to mid-Mar, Mon lunch, Tue & Wed

St-Quay-Portrieux
Ker-Moor (€€)

Striking clifftop hotel with panoramic views over the coastline. The restaurant is renowned for expert seafood cooking and is very popular at lunchtime. Ask about the Taster menus.

✉ 13 rue du Président Le Sénéchal ☎ 02 96 23 50 21 🕐 Closed Christmas–mid-Jan, Sun off-season, Mon lunch

Trégastel
Auberge de la Vieille Eglise (€€)

This charming, flower-covered restaurant stands in the old village a little way inland from the beach resort; worth finding for outstanding cooking in a lovely setting. Best to book.

✉ Place de l'Eglise ☎ 02 96 23 88 31 🕐 Closed Mon, Sun eve

Tréguier
Poissonerie du Trégor (€€)

You can buy fish to take away or eat it upstairs in the tasting rooms at this unusual combination of fishmonger and restaurant. Special children's menus. No puddings.

✉ 2 rue Renan ☎ 02 96 92 30 27 🕐 Tasting rooms daily Jul–Sep

Gourmet Centres

Several sites in Brittany have been selected by the National Council for Culinary Arts as centres of outstanding gourmet excellence (*sites remarquables du goût*). Cancale and Riec-sur-Bélon are singled out for oyster-farming, for example, while the fishing ports of Concarneau, Le Guilvinec and Camaret respectively offer prime tuna, crayfish and trout. Pont-Aven has a celebrated biscuit-making industry. Plougastel is renowned for its strawberries and Redon is famous for its chestnuts.

Ille-et-Vilaine

Sea Salt
Breton butter is always on the table whenever fresh bread is served. Its hidden secret is the fine sea-salt produced in Loire-Atlantique, which characterises many of Brittany's classic biscuits, cakes and pancakes. The salt content in butter varies between 0.5 and 3 per cent, a sharp contrast to the mostly unsalted butter sold elsewhere in France. The saltpans around Guérande produce two types of salt. The coarse grey crystals that form below the waterline are known as *gros sel*, destined for everyday cooking and industrial uses. The more prized *fleurs de sel* are raked from the surface and sold in small packages for speciality cooking and table use. One famous dish is *bar de ligne au sel de Guérande* (sea bass baked in a salt crust). On the reclaimed saltmarsh meadows near Mont-St-Michel, *pré-salé* lamb is raised, with a distinctive salty flavour.

Cancale
Maisons de Bricourt (€€€)
Olivier Roellinger's acclaimed cooking combines the best and freshest regional produce with exotic spices. Three separate locations near Cancale (see also hotel section).
⊠ 1 rue Duguesclin ☎ 02 99 89 64 76 🕓 Closed mid-Dec to mid-Mar, Tue, Wed off-season

Le Surcouf (€€)
One of the best restaurants lining the waterfront. Splendid arrays of seafood, and home-baked buckwheat bread.
⊠ 7 quai Gambetta ☎ 02 99 89 61 75 🕓 Closed mid-Nov–Jan, Wed & Thu off-season

Combourg
L'Ecrivain (€€)
Opposite the church, this good-value place serves a limited but impeccably fresh choice of dishes.
⊠ Place St-Gilduin ☎ 02 99 73 01 61 🕓 Closed early Oct, Feb hols, Thu, Wed & Sun eve off-season

Dinard
Didier Méril (€€)
The dynamic young chef here is definitely on the ascendant, serving talented seafood dishes, along with excellent bread and desserts.
⊠ 6 rue Yves Verney ☎ 02 99 46 95 74 🕓 Late Nov–early Dec, mid-Jan

Fougères
Le Mediéval (€)
An attractive place by the castle for light snacks (*moules frîtes* or pancakes), or inexpensive full meals. Outdoor tables beside the moat.

⊠ Rue Le Bouteiller ☎ 02 99 94 92 59 🕓 Lunch, dinner

Les Voyageurs (€)
Concentrate on the reliable classic cooking here; the urban setting isn't especially charming. Separately managed from the adjacent hotel.
⊠ 10 place Gambetta ☎ 02 99 99 14 17 🕓 Closed Sat lunch, Sun eve

La Guerche-de-Bretagne
La Calèche (€€)
A reliably comfortable restaurant-with-rooms not far from La Roche aux Fées. Bright dining-room. Good-value lunch menus.
⊠ 16 avenue Général Leclerc ☎ 02 99 96 21 63 🕓 Closed early Aug, Fri & Sun eve, Mon

Hédé
Le Genty Home (€€)
Talented regional cooking in a charming flower-decked inn with stone walls and open fires.
⊠ Vallée de Hédé ☎ 02 99 45 46 07 🕓 Closed 2 weeks in Mar, 3 weeks in Nov, Tue eve, Wed

La Vieille Auberge (€€)
Pretty, terraced restaurant in a 17th-century granite house beside a small lake.
⊠ Route de Tinténiac ☎ 02 99 45 46 25 🕓 Closed Jan, Sun eve, Mon

Mont-St-Michel
Château du Bois Guy (€€)
This lovely château is also a hotel. At just 30 minutes from Mont-St-Michel, it's an idyllic place to stop off and eat on the terrace, weather permitting. The dishes use seasonal ingredients with an

individual touch.
✉ 35133 Parigné ☎ 02 99 97
25 76 🕐 Closed Sun eve, Mon

Redon
La Bogue (€€)
Enterprising regional cooking
in a quaint setting near the
town hall. Seasonal chestnut
specialities.
✉ 3 rue des Etats ☎ 02 99 71
12 95 🕐 Closed late Feb, Sun
eve, Thu off-season

Jean-Marc Chandouineau (€€)
An unexpectedly smart
restaurant-with-rooms by
the railway station.
Accomplished, inventive use
of local ingredients.
✉ 10 avenue de la Gare
☎ 02 99 71 02 04 🕐 Closed
early Jan, early May, mid-Aug,
Sat, Sun eve

Rennes
Auberge St-Sauveur (€€)
Set in an ancient timber-
framed building near the
cathedral, this atmospheric
place offers plenty of choice.
Pick your own lobster.
✉ 6 rue St-Sauveur ☎ 02 99
79 32 56 🕐 Closed Sat & Mon
lunch, Sun

Chouin (€€)
A smart restaurant attached
to a fish shop, so there's
plenty of seafood. Good-
value lunch menus.
✉ 12 rue d'Isly ☎ 02 99 30 87
86 🕐 Closed early Aug, Sun,
Mon

Crêperie Ste-Anne (€)
An excellent pancake house
in a handy location for
sightseeing. Generously
filled crêpes are made before
your eyes.
✉ 5 place Ste-Anne ☎ 02 99
79 22 72 🕐 Closed Sun

Four à Ban (€€)
An 18th-century setting
for above-average cooking
using the freshest, seasonal
produce.

✉ 4 rue St-Mélaine ☎ 02 99
38 72 85 🕐 Closed end Jul,
mid-Feb, Sat lunch, Sun

Léon le Cochon (€€)
Sophisticated modern
cooking in a pleasingly rustic
restaurant decked with dried
flowers and chilli peppers.
Unusual offal dishes.
✉ 1 rue du Maréchal-Joffre
☎ 02 99 79 37 54 🕐 Closed
Sun Jul–Aug

St-Malo
À la Duchesse Anne (€€€)
A famous, long-established
restaurant close to the
ramparts that is always busy.
Specialities include lobster
and tarte tatin. No set
menus.
✉ 5 place Guy La Chambre
☎ 02 99 40 85 33 🕐 Closed
Dec–Jan, Mon lunch, Wed, Sun
eve off-season

L'Atré (€€)
An excellent choice if you
find yourself in St-Servan,
with fine views over the
Solidor beach. Wide-ranging
menus.
✉ 7 esplanade St-Menguy,
St-Servan ☎ 02 99 81 68 39
🕐 Closed mid-Dec–Jan, Wed,
eves Sun & Tue off-season

Café de l'Univers (€€)
This characterful intra-muros
bar by the château belongs
to one of St-Malo's oldest
hotels (stylishly refurbished
rooms). Terrace dining in
summer.
✉ Place Chateaubriand
☎ 02 99 40 89 52 🕐 Closed
Wed off-season

Vitré
Taverne de l'Ecu (€€)
Very close to the château,
this quaintly timbered old
inn offers good seafood
specialities at a wide range
of prices.
✉ 12 rue Beaudrairie ☎ 02
99 75 11 09 🕐 Closed Feb,
Easter hols, Wed & Tue eve off-
season

Pancake Paradise
Pancake restaurants are
Brittany's unique 'fast
food' speciality. You'll find
crêperies everywhere, but
standards vary widely –
locals can always tell you
who makes the best
pancakes with the most
generous fillings. Those
deftly produced before
your eyes for a euro or
two at a market stall and
handed to you in a scroll of
paper can be every bit as
delicious as some
elaborate seafood
concoction in a
sophisticated restaurant. A
savoury galette with a
side-salad, followed by a
sweet crêpe is a quick,
satisfying meal, while a
lacy crêpe dentelle can be
eaten as a sweet snack at
any time of day. If you
want to have a shot at
making your own Breton
pancakes, look out for the
special griddle pans and
tools on sale in houseware
shops, including a râteau
(rake) and a spatule (flat
knife). Traditionally, cider is
drunk with pancakes.

Loire-Atlantique

Early Vegetables
Brittany's Ceinture d'Orée in northern Finistère, centred on St-Pol-de-Léon, is France's leading vegetable-growing region. It specialises in *primeurs* (early crops). Globe artichokes, cauliflowers and potatoes thrive in the mild Gulf-Stream climate, along with salad crops, tomatoes and asparagus. Roscoff's famous onion-sellers once plied their wares many miles from home on bicycles throughout the UK. A drive down the Morlaix estuary towards Carentec in September leads past swathes of tall, glaucous, spiky buds as the artichoke crop reaches perfection. Tours around some modern vegetable- and flower-growing farms can be arranged for interested visitors. For more details, contact Pays du Haut-Léon ✉ Place de l'Evêche, St-Pol-de-Léon ☎ 02 98 29 09 09.

La Baule
La Ferme du Grand Clos (€)
This smart farmhouse *crêperie* offers country dishes like *cassoulet* and duck *confit* as well as delicious pancakes.
✉ 52 avenue de Lattre-de-Tassigny ☎ 02 40 60 03 30 🕐 Closed Tue & Wed off-season

Rossini – Hôtel Lutétia (€€)
Classic 1930s décor adds to the atmosphere of this hotel-restaurant. Fillet of beef Rossini is a house speciality; exceptional seafood.
✉ 13 avenue Evens ☎ 02 40 60 25 81 🕐 Closed early Oct, mid-Jan, Sun eve, Tue lunch, Mon off-season

Le Croisic
L'Océan (€€€)
A magnificent waterfront setting adds to the enjoyment of the excellent seafood at this well-managed hotel-restaurant.
✉ Port-Lin ☎ 02 40 62 90 03 🕐 Lunch, dinner

Guérande
Roc-Maria (€)
Charming *crêperie* in a 15th-century building within the town walls. Cosy bedrooms are also available.
✉ 1 rue Vieux Marché aux Grains ☎ 02 40 24 90 51 🕐 Closed mid-Nov to mid-Dec, Wed & Thu off-season

Nantes
Auberge du Château (€€)
Inventive cooking is served in intimate surroundings just opposite the castle.
✉ 5 place de la Duchesse Anne ☎ 02 40 74 31 85 🕐 Closed mid-Aug, Christmas & New Year, Sun, Mon

Café du Marché (€)
This simple formula – a single inexpensive daily menu with three or four starters followed by a dish of the day, proves immensely popular.
✉ 1 rue de Mayence ☎ 02 40 47 63 50 🕐 Weekday lunch only. Closed Aug

Chez l'Huitre (€€)
An atmospheric bistro in the old town specialising in seafood, including oysters and mixed platters.
✉ 5 rue des Petites Ecuries ☎ 02 51 82 02 02 🕐 Closed Sun

La Cigale (€€)
A wonderful *fin-de-siècle* interior with panelling and ceramics is the main attraction of this classic brasserie. Seafood lunches, cakes and after-theatre suppers.
✉ 4 place Graslin ☎ 02 51 84 94 94 🕐 Daily until midnight

Parque Régional de la Brière
Auberge de Kerbourg (€€€€)
One of the most memorable restaurants anywhere in the park, both for its beautifully kept thatch and gardens, and its award-winning cooking.
✉ Route de Guérande, Kerbourg ☎ 02 40 61 95 15 🕐 Closed mid-Dec to mid-Feb, Tue lunch, Sun eve, Mon

Le Nézil (€€)
Nestling in the Parc Régional de Brière this thatched cottage houses a delightful restaurant. There is a good choice of dishes; artichokes, eels, Guinea fowl and frogs' legs all appear on the menu.
✉ St-Lyphard ☎ 02 40 91 41 41 🕐 Closed Sun eve, Mon

Morbihan

Auray
L'Eglantine (€€)
Located down by the old port, this restaurant decked with portraits of Chouan heroes serves up well-prepared Breton classics at fair prices.

✉ Place St-Sauveur, St-Goustan ☎ 02 97 56 46 55
🕐 Closed Wed

Baden
Gavrinis (€€)
A cheerful, family-run hotel bright with flowers, near the shores of the Golfe du Morbihan. The restaurant is highly regarded and offers good-value lunches.

✉ Toulbroch (2km on Vannes road) ☎ 02 97 57 00 82
🕐 Closed mid-Nov–Jan, Sun eve & Mon off-season

Belle-Ile
Roz Avel (€€)
Standing just behind the church in photogenic Sauzon, this is one of Belle-Ile's safest bets for a good meal. Local lamb is on the menu. Tables are set up outside in summer.

✉ Sauzon ☎ 02 97 31 61 48
🕐 Closed Jan–Feb, Wed

Carnac
La Côte (€€)
If you need sustenance while megalith-hunting, try this excellent family-run restaurant for fresh and subtle combinations of taste and texture.

✉ Alignments de Kermario
☎ 02 97 52 02 80 🕐 Closed early Dec, Jan, early Mar, Mon, Sat lunch & Sun eve off-season

Hennebont
Château de Locguénolé (€€€)
Elegant and extremely grand riverside Relais et Châteaux hotel with elaborate and highly regarded cooking.

✉ Route de Port-Louis ☎ 02 97 76 76 76 🕐 Closed Jan to mid-Feb, lunch Mon–Sat, Mon off-season

Ile aux Moines
Les Embruns (€€)
A reliable choice located on one of the islands in the Golfe du Morbihan, regularly visited by boat trips in summer.

✉ Rue du Commerce ☎ 02 97 26 30 86 🕐 Closed early Oct, Jan–Feb, Sun, Wed eve

Locmariaquer
L'Escale (€€)
A glorious waterfront location is the main attraction of this unpretentious hotel. Its covered restaurant terrace overlooks the Golfe du Morbihan.

✉ 2 place Dariorigum
☎ 02 97 57 32 51 🕐 Closed Oct–Mar

Lorient
L'Amphitryon (€€€)
Gourmet diners should track down this small, exclusive temple of gastronomy on the northwest side of town (towards Quimperlé). Seafood specialities.

✉ 127 rue du Colonel Muller
☎ 02 97 83 34 04 🕐 Closed early Jan, early May, early Sep, Sun & Mon off-season

Le Jardin Gourmand (€€€)
This place near the railway station has earned its fine reputation. Elegant setting. Tables outside. Good service.

✉ 46 rue Jules-Simon ☎ 02 97 64 17 24 🕐 Closed Feb hols, early Aug, Sun, Mon

Country Cooking
If traditional home-cooking appeals to you, look out for *fermes auberges* or *auberges du teroir*. Roughly translated as farmhouse inns, these places provide typical country menus using local produce. Ask for a list at any tourist office. Some have accommodation as well, generally fairly simple but sometimes memorably atmospheric.

99

Café Life

Conventional restaurants or *crêperies* are far from Brittany's only eating places. *Brasseries*, cafés and tea-rooms (*salons de thé*) fill in the gaps outside normal mealtimes, offering quiches, salads, cakes and pastries, seafood platters with Muscadet, and sometimes full *menus*. Cafés and bars can provide a much better value breakfast than most hotels too, so if it isn't included in the room price, consider having breakfast elsewhere. In a true French café, customers can spend as long as they want over a single coffee, at least outside mealtimes. In practice, however, you'll certainly feel some pressure to move on or order something more if you're occupying a prime terrace table. If you just want a quick bite, look out for *les snacks* or *casses-croûtes*. Typical snacks are filled baguettes or toasted sandwiches (the classic is a *croque-monsieur*, with cheese and ham, or a *croque-madame*, with cheese and bacon or sausage).

Malestroit
Le Canotier (€)
A romantic split-level restaurant on the market square of a charming historic town. Terrace dining. Good value.

✉ **Place du Dr-Queinnec**
☎ **02 97 75 08 69** ⏰ **Closed Sun eve, Mon**

Port-Louis
La Grève de Locmalo (€)
Well-crafted *crêpes* and tasty fish dishes (especially mussels) are on offer in this bright little stone-built restaurant by the harbour.

✉ **18 bis rue Locmalo** ☎ **02 97 82 48 41** ⏰ **Closed Nov–Mar, Wed eve, Fri lunch & Thu off-season**

Questembert
Le Bretagne (€€€€)
Superb, award-winning cooking at this lovely restaurant-with-rooms.

✉ **13 rue St-Michel** ☎ **02 97 26 11 12** ⏰ **Closed Jan, Tue lunch, Mon off-season**

Quiberon
Le Relax (€€)
Sit outside and admire the sea views and gardens of this pretty restaurant. Enjoy the carefully prepared fish dishes that change according to the season.

✉ **27 boulevard Castéro**
☎ **02 97 50 12 84** ⏰ **Closed Mon**

La Roche-Bernard
Auberge Bretonne (€€€)
Celebrated restaurant-with-rooms with accomplished cuisine. Treat yourself to a dish prepared by one of France's top chefs and chose the number of courses you want according to your appetite, and budget. The service is equally refined. Garden courtyard. Lovely bedrooms.

✉ **2 place du Guesclin**
☎ **02 99 90 60 28** ⏰ **Closed Thu & Mon, Tue, Fri lunch**

Sarzeau
L'Hortensia (€€)
This charming granite house on the Rhuys peninsula offers superb regional cooking in hydrangea-blue dining rooms. Lots of seafood.

✉ **La Grée Penvins** ☎ **02 97 67 42 15** ⏰ **Closed early Mar, late Nov–mid-Dec, Mon & Tue off-season**

La Trinité-sur-Mer
L'Ostréa (€€)
Well-prepared, generously filled seafood platters are served at this little quayside hotel. You can eat on the terrace with sea-views.

✉ **34 cours des Quais**
☎ **02 97 55 73 23** ⏰ **Closed Jan–mid-Feb, Sun eve, Mon off-season**

Vannes
Le Pressoir (€€€)
Renowned restaurant with rustic Louis XIII décor just north of town. Ambitious, wide-ranging menus. Muscadet wines.

✉ **7 rue Hôpital, St-Avé**
☎ **02 97 60 87 63** ⏰ **Closed mid-Mar, early Jul, early Oct, early Jan, Sun eve, Mon, Tue**

Roscanvec (€€)
An inventive selection of dishes are on offer in this fine timbered building situated in a picturesque part of the old town. The principle dining room is on the first floor.

✉ **17 rue Halles** ☎ **02 97 47 15 96** ⏰ **Closed Sun eve, Mon off-season**

Table des Gourmets (€€)
Tasty meals at reasonable prices are served in this restaurant just opposite the town's ramparts. Often exhibits paintings of local artists in the dining room.

✉ **6 rue a le Pontois**
☎ **02 97 47 52 44** ⏰ **Closed Sun eve, Mon lunch, Wed**

Finistère

L'Aber Wrac'h
Baie des Anges (€€–€€€)
A delightful base on one of northwest Finistère's *abers* (drowned valleys). This white-painted building has been stylishly renovated. Wonderful views.

✉ 350 route des Anges
☎ 02 98 04 90 04 🕐 Closed Jan–mid-Feb

Beg-Meil
Belle-Vue (€€)
An attractive, well-kept *Logis* near the beaches of Cap-Coz. Simple, rustic furnishings.

✉ 30 Descente de Belle-Vue, Cap Coz ☎ 02 98 56 00 33
🕐 Closed Nov–Feb

Bénodet
Armoric (€€–€€€)
This welcoming, family-run hotel is spotlessly clean and smartly furnished. The English-speaking owners couldn't be more helpful. Excellent bathrooms and a good breakfast.

✉ 3 rue de Penfoul
☎ 02 98 57 04 03

Sainte-Marine (€€)
A beautifully located hotel-restaurant just across the Odet estuary; chic and stylish with bright, contemporary bedrooms. Always very popular. Book ahead.

✉ 19 rue du Bac, Ste-Marine
☎ 02 98 56 34 79 🕐 Closed mid-Nov to mid-Dec

Brignogan-Plages
Castel Régis (€€)
A wonderful beachfront location distinguishes this well-equipped, peaceful resort hotel.

✉ Promenade du Garo ☎ 02 98 83 40 22 🕐 Closed Oct–Mar

Carentec
Carentec–Patrick Jeffrey (€€€)
Stunning views over the beach and gardens make a fine setting for this palatial restaurant-with-rooms. Several bedrooms have their own balconies.

✉ 20 rue du Kelenn ☎ 02 98 67 00 47 🕐 Closed Jan, mid-Dec

Châteaulin
Au Bon Acceuil (€)
This neat, spacious *Logis* overlooking the River Aulne makes a good touring base for inland Finistère or the Nantes–Brest Canal.

✉ Port-Launay ☎ 02 98 86 15 77 🕐 Closed Jan

Châteauneuf-du-Faou
Relais de Cornouaille (€)
A classic French provincial *Logis* in the town centre. The restaurant is a regular haunt for locals. Handy for touring the Montagnes Noires.

✉ 9 rue Serusier ☎ 02 98 81 75 36 🕐 Closed Oct

Douarnenez
Clos de Vallombreuse (€€–€€€)
Right in the heart of the old town, this secluded mansion has elegant, understated furnishings and a noteworthy restaurant.

✉ 7 rue d'Etienne d'Orves
☎ 02 98 92 63 64

Lampaul-Guimilliau
De l'Enclos (€)
Functional but friendly *Logis* right next to one of Finistère's most famous parish closes.

✉ Route de St-Jacques
☎ 02 98 68 77 08

Prices
Ratings are based on prices per room per night
€   =   up to €50
€€   =   €50–100
€€€ =   over €100

If no closing periods are specified, assume the following hotels stay open all year round. Many of the restaurants listed in Where to Eat and Drink (▶ 92–100) also offer accommodation.

Logis de France
The famous green-and-yellow *Logis de France* 'fireplace' symbol is a beacon of welcome to many a weary traveller in France. This nationwide consortium of around 4,000 modest, privately owned hotels has an inspection system, and members must meet certain standards. That said, individual *Logis* do vary considerably. Indeed a great part of their charm is that, unlike chain hotels, they are family run and have a personal feel. They generally offer good home-cooking too. Prices are inexpensive to moderate, and establishments are graded with 1 to 3 *cheminées* depending on the level of facilities offered. An annual guide with details, prices and maps of all members is available free of charge from the Maison de la France (FGTO) or direct from the Fédération Nationale des Logis de France ✉ 83 avenue d'Italie, 75013 Paris ☎ 01 45 84 70 00; www.logis-de-france.fr

Gîtes de France
A vast range of these immensely popular rural self-catering holiday homes is available to rent in Brittany. Nearly all are privately owned; a few are annexed to hotels, or belong to local councils (*gîtes communaux*). They may be cottages, farmhouses or converted outbuildings, chalets, villas, bungalows or apartments, varying greatly in size, style and standards of luxury. Though self-contained, they may be attached or near to the owner's property, and you may have to share a garden. Bookings can be made directly through the umbrella organisation Gîtes de France ⊠ 59 rue St-Lazare, Paris 75439 ☎ 01 49 70 75 75; www.gites-de-france.fr.

Landerneau
Clos du Pontic (€€)
A quiet, well-equipped *Logis* in an unusual turretted house with modern extensions and lovely gardens. Offers a convenient, self-contained inland touring base.
⊠ **Rue du Pontic** ☎ **02 98 21 50 91**

Locquirec
Grand Hôtel des Bains (€€€)
A truly idyllic coastal setting for a stylishly restored *belle époque* spa hotel with a striking, contemporary interior.
⊠ **15 rue de l'Eglise** ☎ **02 98 67 41 02** ⊙ **Closed Jan–mid-Feb**

Locronan
Manoir de Moëllien (€€–€€€)
This tranquil 17th-century manor has plenty of character, and attractive bedrooms (most in a stable-block annexe).
⊠ **Plonévez-Porzay** ☎ **02 98 92 50 40** ⊙ **Closed Nov–Mar**

Moëlan-sur-Mer
Moulins du Duc (€€–€€€)
Deeply rural luxury hotel in 16th-century watermill. Large, picturesque grounds. Antique furnishings, period character. Good restaurant.
⊠ **Route des Moulins** ☎ **02 98 96 52 52** ⊙ **Closed Jan–Feb, Nov**

Morgat
Julia (€)
A welcoming, well-managed, family-run hotel-restaurant close to the sea. Bright, fresh décor and great home-cooking. A good base on the Crozon peninsula.
⊠ **43 rue du Tréflez** ☎ **02 98 27 05 89** ⊙ **Closed early Nov–Christmas, Jan–late Feb**

Port Manec'h
Ar Men Du (€€)
This small, smartly renovated hotel-restaurant occupies a splendid isolated beachfront location. Bright restaurant with lovely views of a tidal islet; practical, contemporary bedrooms with high-quality fittings.
⊠ **Raguenès-Plage** ☎ **02 98 06 84 22** ⊙ **Closed Oct–Mar (except school and Christmas hols)**

Roscoff
Le Brittany (€€–€€€)
A constant favourite with UK ferry travellers, this tastefully furnished 18th-century manor hotel on the sea-front is sophisticated but welcoming. Good leisure facilities and an excellent restaurant.
⊠ **Boulevard Ste-Barbe** ☎ **02 98 69 70 78** ⊙ **Closed Nov–Mar**

St-Jean du Doigt
Ty Pont (€)
The best sort of family-run *Logis*, offering a friendly welcome, comfortable rooms and good home-cooking near the church. A great touring base or lunch-stop along the Armorique Corniche.
⊠ **Place Robert Le Meur** ☎ **02 98 67 34 06** ⊙ **Closed Nov–Easter (except Jul–Aug)**

Ste-Anne-la-Palud
La Plage (€€€)
A tranquil, up-market hotel-restaurant facing a glorious beach. It appeals mainly to older guests seeking comfort, relaxation and good food.
⊠ **Ste-Anne-la-Palud** ☎ **02 98 92 50 12** ⊙ **Closed Nov–Mar**

Trégunc
Les Grandes Roches (€–€€)
Just 3km east of Concarneau, this rambling old Breton house feels surprisingly rural in extensive park-like grounds.
⊠ **Rue des Grandes Roches** ☎ **02 98 97 62 97** ⊙ **Closed Jan**

Côtes d'Armor

Brélidy
Château de Brélidy (€€–€€€)
A tastefully restored 16th-century manor with a long history. Extensive parkland and river fishing. Elegant, luxuriously furnished interior.
✉ Brélidy ☎ 02 96 95 69 38 🕔 Closed Jan–Easter

Dinan
D'Avaugour (€€€)
Smartly refurbished, this well-run hotel with garden views over the ramparts has stylish rooms and plenty of character. Breakfast only.
✉ 1 place du Champ ☎ 02 96 39 07 49 🕔 Closed mid-Nov–Jan (except Christmas & New Year)

Erquy
Beauséjour (€€)
Reliable, flower-decked *Logis* with sea views not far from the port. Welcoming atmosphere and appetising regional menu. Obligatory half-board in high season.
✉ 21 rue de la Corniche ☎ 02 96 72 30 39 🕔 Closed Christmas–mid-Jan, mid-Feb

Guingamp
Relais du Roi (€€€)
A smart and comfortably modernised hotel-restaurant in an imposing 16th-century building on the market square. Refined cuisine.
✉ 42 place du Centre ☎ 02 96 43 76 62 🕔 Closed early Jan

Paimpol
Repaire du Kerroc'h (€€–€€€)
This historic corsair's house by the port has stylishly refurbished rooms at a good range of prices. Well-regarded restaurant.
✉ 29 quai Morand ☎ 02 96 20 50 13

Perros-Guirec
Manoir du Sphinx (€€€)
An elegant turn-of-the-20th-century building in a spectacular cliff-top location. Light, contemporary interior.
✉ 67 chemin de la Messe ☎ 02 96 23 25 42 🕔 Closed Jan–Feb

Plouer-sur-Rance
Manoir de Rigourdaine (€–€€)
A rambling country house in a rural setting overlooking the Rance. Elegant bedrooms in skilfully converted courtyard buildings. No restaurant, but good value for such high standards.
✉ Route de Langrolay ☎ 02 96 86 89 96 🕔 Closed mid-Nov–Mar

Sables-d'Or-les-Pins
Manoir de la Salle (€€–€€€)
Attractively renovated stone-built manor not far from a lovely section of the Emerald Coast. Games room. No restaurant.
✉ Rue du Lac ☎ 02 96 72 38 29 🕔 Closed Oct–Mar

Trébeurden
Ti al Lannec (€€€)
A long-established place in an enviable location on the Pink Granite Coast. Elegant but welcoming décor. Beautiful grounds and views.
✉ 14 allée de Mezo Guen ☎ 02 96 15 01 01 🕔 Closed mid-Nov to mid-Mar

Tréguier
Kastell Dinec'h (€€)
A comfortably converted manor farmhouse just outside the town. Ornate bedrooms. Good cooking.
✉ Route de Lannion ☎ 02 96 92 49 39 🕔 Closed Jan–Mar, mid-Oct

Chambres d'Hôtes
The French equivalent of what we call bed-and-breakfast in Britain is generally a more peaceful and personal alternative to staying in a hotel, though not necessarily a great deal cheaper. Some *chambres d'hôtes* are quite luxurious – you may even stay in a château or manor-house – but they do not offer hotel facilities or services. You have a chance to meet your hosts (some speak good English, but it's obviously an opportunity to practise your French). Some provide a *table d'hôte* dinner, by prior arrangement. Gîtes de France represents many *chambres d'hôtes*, and grades them with an ear of corn symbol according to their standards of comfort and facilities (1–4 *epis*).

Ille-et-Vilaine

Staying in Style

Around 30 of Brittany's most memorable and distinctive hotels are listed in a publication called *Hôtels de Charme et de Caractère en Bretagne*, which you can pick up free of charge at any tourist office. (Many are recommended in these pages, incidentally.) Also available free (though postage is charged) are several Châteaux guides, such as *Relais & Châteaux, Châteaux & Hôtels de France, Bienvenue au Château, Château Acceuil*. These provide top-range accommodation and often gourmet dining in splendid historic settings. Most are understandably expensive, but some are surprisingly good value. Grandes Etapes Françaises and Relais du Silence hotels also guarantee a characterful stay in peaceful surroundings.

Cancale
Continental (€€–€€€)
This charming hotel-restaurant located on the waterfront is one of the best places to savour some of Cancale's famous oysters.
✉ **4 quai Thomas** ☎ **02 99 89 60 16** 🕐 **Closed mid-Nov–Mar**

Pointe de Grouin (€€)
A solid stone *Logis* on a spectacular promontory overlooking the bird-sanctuary islet of Ile des Landes. Overrun with day-trippers at lunchtime, but lovely once the crowds depart. Good traditional cooking.
✉ **Pointe de Grouin** ☎ **02 99 89 60 55** 🕐 **Closed mid-Nov–Mar**

Châteaubourg
Ar Milin (€€–€€€)
A large, well-equipped hotel-restaurant housed in a converted mill. The good leisure facilities include tennis, horse riding, and cycling, and the hotel is set in extensive wooded riverside grounds. A handy touring base for the eastern Marches.
✉ **30 rue de Paris** ☎ **02 99 00 30 91** 🕐 **Closed early Dec–early Jan**

Pen-Roc (€€)
This delightfully converted farmhouse has its own chapel and enjoys a peaceful rural setting just 20 minutes' drive from Rennes. The high-quality cooking.is served in stylish surroundings by very courteous staff.
✉ **La Peinière, St-Didier** ☎ **02 99 00 33 02** 🕐 **Closed Christmas & New Year**

Combourg
Du Château (€€–€€€)
A comfortable superior *Logis* near the castle and lake. Smart classic and traditional décor. The restaurant turns out reliable cooking.
✉ **1 place Chateaubriand** ☎ **02 99 73 00 38** 🕐 **Closed mid-Dec to mid-Jan**

Dinard
Grand Hôtel Barrière de Dinard (€€€)
This grand seafront institution dates from Dinard's heyday, and still occupies a prime location at the mouth of the Rance. Facilities are predictably impressive.
✉ **46 avenue George V** ☎ **02 99 88 26 26** 🕐 **Closed Nov–Mar**

Printania (€€)
Waitresses dress in Breton costume at this delightfully furnished and idiosyncratic hotel with marvellous views over the Rance estuary.
✉ **5 avenue George V** ☎ **02 99 46 13 07** 🕐 **Closed mid-Nov–Mar**

Reine Hortense (€€€€)
A refined *fin-de-siècle* residence with lovely views of the main beach from its peaceful gardens. Breakfast terrace. No restaurant.
✉ **19 rue Malouine** ☎ **02 99 46 54 31** 🕐 **Closed mid-Nov–Mar**

Fougères
Balzac (€)
A simple but charming old granite house on the semi-pedestrianised main street of the upper town. Attractively refurbished bedrooms.
✉ **15 rue Nationale** ☎ **02 99 99 42 46**

Hédé
Hostellerie du Vieux Moulin (€€)
Charming, creeper-covered building with a bell tower and bedrooms overlooking colourful gardens.

✉ **La Vallée du Moulin** ☏ **02 99 45 45 70** 🕐 **Closed late Oct, Jan**

Rennes
Lecoq-Gadby (€€€)
In a quiet residential district just outside the historic old town, this tastefully refined hotel has the air of a private home. Period furnishings and *objets d'art*. Pretty gardens.

✉ **156 rue d'Antrain**
☏ **02 99 38 05 55**

St-Malo
L'Ascott (€€–€€€)
Elegantly renovated 19th-century town house in quiet St-Servan. Bedrooms are individually designed in dashing colour schemes with high-quality fabrics and fittings. Breakfast served in gardens in summer.

✉ **35 rue du Chapitre, St-Servan** ☏ **02 99 81 89 93**

Le Beaufort (€€–€€€)
Exceptionally chic décor in cool, muted tones. Welcoming atmosphere. Wonderful sea views from dining room and front bedrooms.

✉ **25 Chausée de Sillon**
☏ **02 99 40 99 99**

Les Charmettes (€)
Charming *pension* overlooking the sea near Paramé.

✉ **64 boulevard Hébert**
☏ **02 99 56 07 31**

Le Cunningham (€€–€€€)
A new venture in a stylishly renovated 17th-century house near the ferry terminal. Spacious, exotic bedrooms. Lovely marina views.

✉ **9 place M Duchesne, St-Servan** ☏ **02 99 21 33 33**
🕐 **Closed Nov–Mar**

La Rance (€€)
A thoroughly civilised little place with estuary views at Port Solidor. Clean, well-equipped bedrooms. Courteous welcome. No restaurant.

✉ **15 quai Sébastopol, St-Servan** ☏ **02 99 81 78 63**

Le Valmarin (€€–€€€)
A charming old *malouinière* (corsair's home) in St-Servan. Though elegant, this place has a very relaxing atmosphere with peaceful gardens. No restaurant.

✉ **7 rue Jean XXIII, St-Servan** ☏ **02 99 81 94 76** 🕐 **Closed sometimes off-season (call to check)**

St-Meloir-des-Ondes
Tirel-Guerin (€€–€€€)
An old railway hotel, stylishly modernised and expanded into a very comfortable, well-equipped hotel-restaurant. Indoor pool. Excellent cooking.

✉ **Gare de la Gouesnière**
☏ **02 99 89 10 46** 🕐 **Closed mid-Dec to mid-Jan**

Vitré
Petit-Billot (€)
Inexpensive set menus in this hotel in the town centre. The restaurant nextdoor complements the hotel

✉ **5 place Général Leclerc**
☏ **02 99 75 02 10** 🕐 **Closed Christmas & New Year**

Le Vivier-sur-Mer
Bretagne (€€)
Recently renovated, this traditional, inexpensive *Logis* is in a fine position overlooking the Baie de Mont-St-Michel. Sauna and gym, and a panoramic restaurant.

✉ **Rond-point du Centre**
☏ **02 99 48 91 74** 🕐 **Closed mid-Nov–Mar**

Chain Hotels
Motel-style accommodation is increasing all over France, generally conveniently located for motorists on major routes or on the outskirts of large towns and ports. The experience offered is fairly impersonal and formulaic, but chain hotels do provide predictably reliable standards of clean, modern facilities and on-site parking. Some (such as Campanile) are renowned for good-value restaurants offering regional cooking. They can be a great boon to travellers, especially for families, or late at night. They are easy to book at short notice via the internet by using a credit card. Most of the cheapest chain hotels (such as Formule 1) are unstaffed at night and offer less security (guests are admitted by credit card). Other budget or moderately priced chains include Balladins B&B Hôtel, Etap, Ibis and Clarine.

Loire-Atlantique

Camping and Caravanning

This is an immensely popular way of taking a holiday in Brittany, for French families as well as foreign tourists. Just about every French community has some sort of camping facility, though many are on the coast – these get completely packed during the summer holidays. All tourist offices can supply a list of local sites. *Camping sauvage* (outside designated sites) is generally illegal or frowned on in France, and may involve you in an unpleasant encounter with an irate farmer (and his dog or shotgun), so always ask permission before you set up camp on private land. Most campsites are open only in the summer months (Easter to September). Rates for tents and caravans are roughly the same. Sites are officially graded 1–4 stars, but many specialist guides available in bookstores select and grade campsites. Camping Plus en Bretagne is a leading chain of around 35 high-quality 3- and 4-star sites in Brittany ✉ BP 28 - 29740 Plobannalec ☎ 02 98 87 87 86; www.campingplus.fr

Batz-sur-Mer

Le Lichen de la Mer (€€–€€€)

On the main seafront road just outside the resort, this solid, traditional hotel has a wonderful panorama of the Côte Sauvage.

✉ Baie du Manérick
☎ 02 40 23 91 92

La Baule

Castel Marie-Louise (€€€)

One of La Baule's most exclusive hotels, an imposing *belle époque* mansion set in immaculate gardens. Sumptuous, formal décor. Acclaimed restaurant.

✉ 1 avenue Andrieu
☎ 02 40 11 48 38 🕐 Closed mid-Dec–Jan

St-Christophe (€€–€€€)

In a quiet residential street, this creeper-covered amalgam of several early 20th-century villas has an elegantly furnished period interior. Good family atmosphere.

✉ Place Notre-Dame
☎ 02 40 62 40 00

St-Pierre (€–€€)

A charming, friendly B&B with prettily decorated rooms. For such a central location, prices are very reasonable. Excellent breakfast.

✉ 124 avenue de Lattre de Tassigny ☎ 02 40 24 05 41

Brière

La Mare aux Oiseaux (€€–€€€)

A typical Brière thatched cottage with charming, stylish bedrooms. Pretty gardens; interesting regional cooking (pike, eel, duck etc). Children's menus.

✉ 162 Ile de Fedrun ☎ 02 40 88 53 01 🕐 Closed Jan–Mar

Le Croisic

Fort de l'Océan (€€€)

This sophisticated place overlooking the far end of the Croisic peninsula attracts a trendy clientele for its designer interior and fashionable restaurant. Glorious views.

✉ Pointe du Croisic
☎ 02 40 15 77 77

Nantes

L'Hôtel (€€)

Neat, chic, practically designed rooms aimed at business travellers in a modern block opposite the château. No restaurant.

✉ 6 rue Henri IV ☎ 02 40 29 30 31 🕐 Closed Christmas & New Year

Pornichet

Sud-Bretagne (€€–€€€)

A gorgeously individual hotel, full of quirky charm and character, but relaxing and comfortable too. Entertaining bedrooms.

✉ 42 boulevard de la République ☎ 02 40 11 65 00

Villa Flornoy (€€)

Just a block or so back from the beach in a quiet side-street by the town hall, this refined, civilised villa has elegantly decorated bedrooms. Pleasant, helpful service.

✉ 7 avenue Flornoy ☎ 02 40 11 60 00 🕐 Closed Jan

St-Marc-sur-Mer

De la Plage (€€)

Monsieur Hulot's holiday hotel is still a seaside classic in a small, traditional resort southwest of St-Nazaire. Good restaurant.

✉ 37 rue du Commandant Charcot ☎ 02 40 91 99 01 🕐 Closed Jan

Morbihan

Belle-Ile-en-Mer
La Desirade (€€–€€€)
A village-like complex of accommodation units in gardens around a heated pool, decorated in a variety of styles.
✉ **Le Petit Cosquet, Bangor**
☎ **02 97 31 70 70** ◐ **Closed Oct**

Billiers
Domaine de Rochevilaine (€€€)
Romantic luxury hideaway in converted coastguard buildings. The setting is truly spectacular and the atmosphere relaxing. Highly regarded restaurant.
✉ **Pointe de Pen Lan**
☎ **02 97 41 61 61**

Carnac
Hostellerie des Ajoncs d'Or (€€)
Delightful stone farmhouse with pretty gardens in a tiny hamlet just outside the town. Cosy, rustic interior. Regional cooking.
✉ **Route de Plouharnel, Kerbachique** ☎ **02 97 52 32 02**
◐ **Closed mid-Oct–Mar**

Des Rochers (€€)
A bright, cheerful resort hotel in a prime location near the yacht club. Bay windows and balconies take advantage of the views. Good value in a somewhat overpriced resort.
✉ **6 boulevard de la Base Nautique** ☎ **02 97 52 10 09**
◐ **Closed Oct–Mar**

Locmariaquer
Les Trois Fontaines (€€)
Very close to the main megalith site, this comfortable, spacious place has light, elegant bedrooms, some with sea views.
✉ **Route d'Auray** ☎ **02 97 57 42 70** ◐ **Closed mid-Nov–Mar**

Pénestin
Loscolo (€€)
A headland charmer on a quiet, scenic beach near the mouth of the Vilaine. Friendly and well-kept.
✉ **Pointe de Loscolo**
☎ **02 99 90 31 90** ◐ **Closed Nov–Mar**

Quiberon
La Petite Sirène (€€)
A moderately priced option near the thalassotherapy centre. Sea views and decent meals; buffet breakfast.
✉ **15 boulevard René Cassin**
☎ **02 97 50 17 34** ◐ **Closed mid-Oct to mid-Mar**

La Roche-Bernard
Auberge des Deux Magots (€–€€)
Pretty stone-built restaurant with rooms on a quiet square near the town hall. Classic, traditionally furnished bedrooms.
✉ **Place du Bouffray**
☎ **02 99 90 60 75** ◐ **Closed Christmas & New Year**

Manoir du Rodoir (€€)
A stone-built country house set back from the road in substantial grounds. Tastefully furnished.
✉ **Route de Nantes** ☎ **02 99 90 82 68** ◐ **Closed Christmas & New Year**

Vannes
Le Roof (€€–€€€)
A modern hotel in a waterfront setting down by the canalised port. Good facilities and spacious, comfortable rooms. Polished but friendly service.
✉ **Presqu'île de Conleau**
☎ **02 97 63 47 47**

Hostels
Most sizeable towns have a hostel or two offering simple dormitory accommodation to travellers of any age for under 15 euros per night. Official youth hostels are called *auberges de jeunesse* in France, though they may belong to one of several different organisations. To stay at these, you must be a member of an affiliated or international hostelling organisation (you can usually purchase a membership card on arrival in any hostel). Several hostels in Brittany are attractively located (such as at Concarneau and Trébeuden), though most tend to be out of the centre of town. University towns sometimes have halls of residence (*foyers*) available during vacation periods. *Gîtes d'étapes* are an inexpensive form of accommodation designed for walkers or cyclists. An annual guide is produced by Gîtes de France (*Gîtes d'Etapes et de Séjour*).

Food Products

Food Markets

Markets are one of the great pleasures of visiting France. Nearly every sizeable town has a weekly open-air produce market, and larger communities may have daily covered markets (*les halles*). Buying from markets is a much more interesting, colourful and personal experience, and the merchandise is generally both cheaper and fresher. It's perfect for picnic fodder or self-catering while you're in France, though supermarket packaging is more suitable for foods you want to keep for a while, or bring home with you. The regional tourist office produces an annually updated list of times and places for Breton fairs and markets, including specialist and seasonal ones.

Seafood

La Forêt-Fouesnant
Les Viviers de la Forêt

A grand array of oysters, crabs, clams, mussels and *langoustines* awaits visitors to this shellfish farm on a sheltered harbour next to the 1,000-berth yacht marina. Direct sales.

✉ **Le Vieux Port** ☎ 02 98 56 96 68

Riec-sur-Bélon
Huitrières du Château de Bélon

Long-established family-run oyster farm on the Bélon estuary. Guided tours for groups; direct sales.

✉ **Riec-sur-Bélon** ☎ 02 98 06 90 58

Roscoff
Algoplus

Seaweeds are processed into multifarious edible, cosmetic and pharmaceutical products at this enterprising firm. Free guided tours of the production plant during the summer.

✉ **Shop: 2 quai Charles de Gaulle** ☎ 02 98 61 14 16

Biscuits, cakes, etc

Concarneau
Georges Larnicol

Typical Breton biscuits, sweets and chocolates are displayed at this attractive shop in the old walled town. There's another branch in Quimper at 14 rue des Boucheries (☎ 02 98 95 88 22).

✉ **9 rue Vauban, Ville Close** ☎ 02 98 60 46 87

Dinan
Les Gavottes

Easy to spot by the tourist office, this attractive place specialises in *crêpes dentelle*, made to a Quimper recipe. A wide range of other cakes, biscuits, chocolates and sweets are on sale too. Free tastings.

✉ **9 rue du Château** ☎ 02 96 87 06 48

Locmariaquer
La Trinitaine

Nearly 20 retail outlets of this large biscuit factory are scattered around Brittany (mostly in Morbihan). Besides cakes and biscuits, they sell all kinds of regional foods – honey, jam, sweets, liqueurs and preserves, etc.

✉ **Route de Crac'h, St-Philibert** ☎ 02 97 55 02 04

Pleyben
Chocolatier Chatillon

Opposite Pleyben's famous calvary, this long-established *chocolatier* invites visitors to watch mouth-watering chocolates and biscuits being made. Film-show, exhibition and tastings.

✉ **Pleyben** ☎ 02 98 26 63 77

Pléneuf-Val-André
La Crêperie

Visitors to this *crêpe* factory can sample the products before buying.

✉ **ZA Le Poirier, St-Alban** ☎ 02 96 32 98 06

Pont-Aven
Les Délices de Pont-Aven

The famous *galettes de Pont-Aven* are made with specially churned Breton butter, and sold in beautifully designed and highly collectable tins all over Brittany. Visits July and August.

✉ **ZA de Kergazuel; shop: 1 quai Theodore Botrel** ☎ 02 98 06 05 87; shop: 02 98 06 00 49

Plouescat
Miellerie de la Côte des Légendes
Honey products and *chouchenn* for sale at this bee-keeping farm not far from the sea. Apiary exhibition and tastings.
✉ **Kerscouarnec** ☎ **02 98 69 88 93**

Savoury products

Goulien
Cap'Helix
An edible snail farm. Guided tours show how they are raised and processed into a variety of tins, jars and packets. Clams and other regional produce also.
✉ **Bréharadec** ☎ **02 98 70 25 83**

Kerhinet
Maison des Saveurs et de l'Artisanat
Guérande salt, samphire and many other delicacies of the Brière region are available at this appealing thatched cottage shop in the heart of the regional park. Crafts and paintings by local artists too.
✉ **Kerhinet** ☎ **02 40 61 95 53**

Pouldreuzic
Jean Hénaff Production
Pâté du Mataf (made of pure pork) is the speciality here. Still sold in distinctive blue tins, it originated in 1914, and was once a staple foodstuff for any Breton sailor.
✉ **Pouldreuzic** ☎ **02 98 51 53 53**

Quiberon
Conserverie La Belle-Iloise
One of Brittany's best-known brands of canned fish. These speciality products are sold in attractive tins. Guided tours and tastings at the factory shop. Over a dozen branches throughout Brittany,
✉ **ZA Plein Ouest** ☎ **02 97 50 08 77**

Alcoholic drinks

Lannion
Warenghem Bretagne
A Breton brand of malt whisky is distilled here. Tours and tastings (Jun–Aug). *Pommeau* (sparkling apple wine) and *fine de Bretagne* (brandy) are on sale at the factory shop.
✉ **Route de Guingamp** ☎ **02 96 37 00 08**

Morlaix
Brasserie Coreff
Four types of real barley beers are made at the Deux-Rivières Brewery in an old rope factory. The Coreff label is a sign of quality. Guided tours in summer, followed by a tasting.
✉ **1 place de la Madeleine** ☎ **02 98 63 41 92**

La Cave des Chouchenn
Chouchenn is a classic Breton drink rather like mead, based on fermented fruit and honey. Tours and tastings in summer (call ahead). Speciality honeys, too.
✉ **Plouégat-Moysan (off N12 17km east of Morlaix)** ☎ **02 98 79 21 25**

Pleudihen-sur-Rance
Musée de la Pomme et du Cidre
This family-run cider-farm (open morning only) is one of the most widely publicised *cidreries* in the Rance Valley. Buy an award-winning product to take home.
✉ **Pleudihen-sur-Rance** ☎ **02 96 83 20 78**

St-Lyphard
Brasserie de la Brière
Classic real ales (blonde, amber, white and organic) are produced at this attractive little micro-brewery in one of the prettiest villages in the Brière Regional Park. Tours and tastings.
✉ **Le Nézyl** ☎ **02 40 91 33 62**

Breton and Loire Wines
Very little wine is produced in Brittany, but the Rhuys peninsula (Morbihan) produces a notoriously strong brew. It's said you need three people and a wall to help you drink it – one to pour it out, one either side to stop you keeling over and the wall behind to prop you up. The vineyards of the Loire produce dry white Muscadet, Gros-Plant and Coteaux d'Ancenis, all good accompaniments to seafood, and often used as a basic ingredient of the sauce for *moules marinières*. One of the best places to buy Loire wines is the Maison des Vins, at La Haie-Fouassière, 20km southeast of Nantes (✉ Bellevue ☎ 02 40 36 90 10), which has over 200 selected estate-bottled wines in stock (free admission; tasting room).

Gifts and Souvenirs

Antiques

Brittany's rural traditions have survived longer than in some parts of France, and many solid old pieces of country furniture can still be found, including linen presses, box beds and marriage chests. Smaller items like butter moulds, decorated wooden spoons, platters, etc can often be tracked down in *bric-à-brac* shops, flea markets and antiques fairs. Several specialists sell marine antiques (barometers, lamps, etc). Many attractive reproductions are available in souvenir shops. A well-organised list of antique dealers and art galleries entitled *Antiquaires, Galeries & Métiers d'Art*, is available in tourist offices.

Craft Villages

St-Méloir-des-Ondes, near Dol-de-Bretagne, has a cluster of artisans' workshops, including potters, basket-makers and a glass-blowing studio. In Camaret, on the Crozon peninsula, nine different art galleries are promoted together as Les Artistes de Camaret. Locronan has many lovely shops selling a great variety of beautiful fabrics, table linen, ceramics and other artefacts eg Les Maison des Artisans (✉ Place de l'Eglise ☎ 02 98 91 70 11). At Pont-Scorff near Lorient, many craftworkers occupy courtyard premises in 17th-century houses called the Cour des Métiers d'Art.

Antiques

Rochefort-en-Terre
Au Bon Vieux Temps
Antiques, bygones and bric-à-brac on display in a vast covered area.
✉ **Route de Malansac**
☎ **02 97 43 32 73**

Soudan
L'Occasion Soudanaise
Country furniture, antique glassware and many small items at this interesting place east of Châteaubriant.
✉ **Route de Laval** ☎ **02 40 28 65 96**

Beauty products

La Gacilly
Yves Rocher
This familiar brand of health and beauty products based on natural ingredients is on sale at the Yves Rocher headquarters near Rennes. Film-show and exhibition.
✉ **La Gacilly** ☎ **02 99 08 35 84**

Books and Music

Quimper
Keltia Musique
A huge range of Breton and Celtic folk music recordings.
✉ **1 place au Beurre**
☎ **02 98 95 95 45 82**

Rennes
Cooperative Breizh
Books, posters, and Breton/Celtic music.
✉ **17 rue Penhoët** ☎ **02 99 79 01 87**

Crafts

Cancale
Bazar Parisien
An attractive range of crafts, gifts, souvenirs and houseware opposite the church on the main square.
✉ **42 rue du Port** ☎ **02 99 89 62 97**

Corps Nuds
Ateliers Helmbold
A specialist glassworks studio southeast of Rennes. Besides restoration of antique stained glass, imaginative contemporary works are on display. Decorative household objects, painting on glass, mirrors etc.
✉ **Le Choizel** ☎ **02 99 44 12 37**

Landerneau
Comptoir des Produits Bretons
A delightful shop for presents and mementoes, with a huge range of quality Breton crafts and regional products, including paintings, sculptures, food specialities books and music recordings. There's another branch in Quimper, 7 rue du Guéodet.
✉ **Quai de Cornouaille**
☎ **02 98 21 35 93**

Quimper
Faïencerie d'Art Breton
A partnership of local ceramic artists with generations of experience behind them, producing hand-decorated pieces in typical Quimper style.
✉ **34 rue Marcel Paul**
☎ **02 98 52 85 28**

HB Henriot
Brittany's leading *faïencerie* featuring classic handpainted *paysanne* designs in the huge showroom. Factory visits – you can take a 'Petit Train' from outside the cathedral that takes you on a guided tour of Quimper and HB Henriot (€3)
✉ **Rue Haute, Locmaria**
☎ **02 98 90 09 36**

Fashion

Accessories

Asserac
Maurice Besulau
Interesting selection of hand-crafted leatherware. Clogs, sandals, bags etc.
✉ 3 place de l'église
☎ 02 40 01 70 89

Callac
Tannerie de Callac
Fish leather is the unusual speciality of this outlet southwest of Guingamp. Beautifully crafted belts, purses, wallets, gloves and handbags are on sale here.
✉ ZA de Kerguiniou
☎ 02 96 45 50 68

Breton classics

Bénodet
Duck-Jibe
Look out for leading Breton clothing brands like Armor-Lux, Guy Cotten and Kana-Beach leisurewear.
✉ 14 avenue Plage
☎ 02 98 57 24 01

Quimper
Au Costume Breton
Breton vests and T-shirts, traditional costumes, coiffes, dolls, etc.
✉ 11 rue Rene Madec
☎ 02 98 95 19 11

Pléstin-les-Grèves
Angora de France
One of France's last remaining angora farms in a handsome turreted château. Visitors can admire the goats and see how they are raised, then inspect the products made from their silky wool (waistcoats, scarves, gloves etc). Mail order service.
✉ Château de Coat-Carric
☎ 02 96 35 62 49 🕐 Daily Mon–Sat 2–6

Pont l'Abbé
Le Minor
The town's traditional hand-embroidered linen is on sale here, along with Breton outdoor and sailing gear (*kabig* capes, jerseys, etc).
✉ 5 quai St-Laurent ☎ 02 98 87 07 22

Outdoor and Sportswear

Arzon
Le Navalo
Swimwear and other leisure clothes, plus beach games and maritime souvenirs.
✉ Pointe de Port Navalo
☎ 02 97 53 72 60

Concarneau
Moussaillon
Look out for the classic fisherman's oilskin sou'wester here, usually in bright yellow.
✉ Avenue Biele, Seld-Zenne
☎ 02 98 97 09 22

St-Malo
Comptoir de la Mer
About 40 branches of this maritime co-operative lie scattered around the ports of Brittany, selling a wide range of specialist clothing, safety equipment, chandlery and nautical souvenirs aimed at sailing and fishing fans.
✉ 3 & 10 avenue F Roosevelt
☎ 02 99 56 13 38

Clogs

Camor
Au Sabot Camorien
Watch clogs being made at Morbihan's last-remaining workshop near Baud, and see an exhibition about clog-making. Lots on sale.
✉ Route d'Auray ☎ 02 97 39 28 64

Sailor Gear
Brittany's maritime traditions have influenced Breton clothing, now just as popular with landlubbers as with sailors. Besides being strong, warm and comfortable, these practical all-weather garments are stylish and fashionable too. Chic stripes in red and navy characterise many Breton sweaters, typically buttoned at the left shoulder. Look for the brands Saint James and Armor-Lux (✉ 60 bis rue Guy Autret ☎ 02 98 90 05 29). Fisherman's reefers, brightly coloured oilskins and the famous Rosbraz sailing jacket (Guy Cotten) are classic items to look out for. Waterproof *vestes de quart* (sea jackets) are widely used by keen sailors – their fluorescent colours are an important safety feature. In Quimper, look out for a *kabig* or heavy outdoor cape with decorative scallop fastenings, suitable for men, women or children.

Children's Attractions

Buckets and Spades

The best place by far to take children in Brittany is to the beach and let them experience the time-honoured pleasures of building sandcastles and exploring rock-pools. As those huge tides recede, a wonderland of marine wildlife is revealed as shellfish pop up mysteriously from the freshly scrubbed sand. Often whole Breton families together head for prized hunting grounds with shrimping nets, rakes and buckets in search of cockles, clams and crabs. Apart from the cost of ice-cream, these amusements are entirely free. But if enthusiasm for such simple pleasures wanes, there are always lighthouses to climb, seaside castles to visit and dozens of boat-trips.

Parc de Préhistoire de Bretagne

In this 20-ha wooded park, with its lakes and disused slate quarries, prehistoric times in Brittany is explained to you in six different languages. Follow the marked path and discover through life-size models and scenes the life of the dinosaurs and the evolution of man.
✉ **Malansac (2km from Rochefort-en-Terre)**
☎ **02 97 43 34 17**

Amusement/Theme parks

Aquarive
A wave-pool, slides and waterfalls at this waterpark on the banks of the Odet.
✉ **Route de Kerogan, Creac'h Gwen, Quimper** ☎ **02 98 52 00 15**

La Récré
A 10-ha leisure park near Brest. Go-karts, dodgems, waterslides and a railway in wooded parkland with a lake.
✉ **Milizac** ☎ **02 98 07 95 59**

Les Balnéides
Indoor waterpark with the longest waterslide in Brittany.
✉ **Allée de Loc'hilaire, Fouesnant** ☎ **02 98 56 18 19**

Le Village Gaulois
Over 20 Gallic-themed activities and games in a reconstructed village.
✉ **Pleumeur-Bodou (10km from Lannion)** ☎ **02 96 91 83 95**

Parc du Golfe
Leisure complex by the waterfront offering an aquarium, a butterfly house and a new Musée de la Marine. Good for wet days.
✉ **Port de Conleau, Vannes** ☎ **02 97 46 01 02**

Aquaria/Zoo parks

La Bourbansais
A zoo park in the grounds of an imposing 16th-century château, plus a maze, a miniature railway and falconry displays.
✉ **Pleugueneuc** ☎ **02 99 69 40 07**

La Ferme du Monde
Animals from five continents roam freely through the confines of this 25-ha site.
✉ **Carentoir** ☎ **02 99 93 70 71**

Grand Aquarium
Colourful fish; Nautibus ride to the ocean bed.
✉ **Avenue du Général Patton, St-Malo** ☎ **02 99 21 19 00**

Insectarium
Close encounters with creepy crawlies.
✉ **Rue du Stade, Lizio** ☎ **02 97 74 99 12**

Océanopolis (➤ 21)

Océarium (➤ 71)

Parc de Branféré
Some 1,500 animals are allowed to wander at will through this attractively landscaped 35-ha park.
✉ **Le Guerno** ☎ **02 97 42 94 66**

Planète Aquarium (➤ 33)

Tropical Parc
Animals, birds and exotic vegetation mingle with Asian-style temples and a Mexican desert.
✉ **St-Jacut-les-Pins** ☎ **02 99 71 91 98**

Museums
Musée des Poupées (➤ 85)

Musée du Costume Breton
A charming collection of china dolls in traditional Breton costumes.
✉ **Ste-Anne-d'Auray** ☎ **02 97 57 68 80**

Victor Pléven
Visit the world's biggest cod-fishing trawler to discover the life and work of the Newfoundland fishermen.
✉ **Base de Sous Marins de Keroman, Lorient** ☎ **02 97 88 15 12**

Nightlife and Culture

Casinos

Casino Barrière de Dinard
Dinard's waterfront casino (1911) harks back to its *belle époque* heyday.
✉ **6 avenue Pierre Loti**
☎ **02 99 16 30 30**

Casino de La Baule
Blackjack and bingo in the smartest part of the resort.
✉ **Esplanade Lucien Barrière**
☎ **02 40 11 48 28**

Clubs and Pubs

Morlaix
Tempo Piano Bar
Cool, lively harbourside bar with regular jazz and blues.
✉ **Quai de Tréguier** ☎ **02 98 63 29 11**

Ty Coz
A quaintly timbered hostelry popular with locals.
✉ **10 Venelle au Beurre**
☎ **02 98 88 07 65**

Rennes
Club Ubu
Live, large-scale music gigs at the same venue as Brittany's National Theatre.
✉ **1 rue St-Helier** ☎ **02 99 30 31 68**

Le Barantic
Live music for a young, studenty crowd. Often busy.
✉ **Rue St-Michel** ☎ **02 99 79 29 24**

St-Malo
Cunningham's Bar
A popular meeting and drinking place down by the marina. Nautical décor.
✉ **Port de Bas-Sablons**
☎ **02 99 81 48 08**

L'Escalier
The place to head if you enjoy dancing.

✉ **La Buzardière, just outside St-Malo** ☎ **02 99 81 65 56**

Vannes
Pub Swansea
Traditional Breton bar; you can hear 'Bretonne' spoken.
✉ **3 rue du Four** ☎ **02 97 42 74 92**

Concerts

Nantes
Cité des Congrès
Regular concert programmes by its resident Orchestre National des Pays de la Loire and visiting musicians.
✉ **5 rue de Valmy** ☎ **02 51 88 20 00**

Theatre and Cinema

Brest
Quartz
Avant-garde fringe theatre at the home of Cinémathèque de Bretagne.
✉ **Avenue Georges Clémenceau** ☎ **02 98 44 24 96**

Morlaix
Le Théâtre du Pays de Morlaix
Hosts plays, local and world music, films and ballet.
✉ **20 rue Gambetta** ☎ **02 98 15 22 77**

Rennes
L'Arvor
Subtitled *version originale* films are sometimes shown.
✉ **29 rue d'Antrain** ☎ **02 99 38 72 40**

Theatre National de Bretagne
A varied programme of seasonal productions (mid-Oct to mid-Jun).
✉ **1 rue St-Helier** ☎ **02 99 31 12 31**

Themed Walking
Coastal paths, canal towpaths and forest trails provide plenty of varied terrain for walkers in Brittany. One of the most famous routes is the *Sentier des Douaniers* (customs officers' path), dating from the late 18th century to prevent smuggling. Restored in the 1980s, it gives access to the entire Breton coast from Cancale to Brière. Another well-known walk is the Tro-Breiz, a medieval pilgrimage route linking the shrines of the seven founding saints, which lie scattered across a wide area from St-Malo to Quimper. Shorter routes are based on Brittany's architectural or cultural heritage, such as the Route des Phares et Balises (lighthouses and beacons) around Brest, the Route du Cidre in Cornouaille, or Emerald Eyes, following Impressionist painters along the Emerald Coast.

Sport

Breton Games
Like most Celtic regions, Brittany loves competitive activities. Trials of strength and team games play an important role in community life, and sometimes feature in summer festivals. Breton wrestling *(ar gouren)* is rather like judo, with loose clothing and ritual kissing. Other traditional games include *tire-baton*, where the contestants try to lift each other with a pole, and the Breton versions of hockey and rugby.

Watersports
Brittany's local and regional tourist offices can supply information about a varied range of watery activities. The *Passion Plage* network of over 30 Breton coastal resorts gives some assurance of high-quality facilities and safety surveillance.

Cycling
Most tourist offices can provide lists of cycling routes and bike-hire centres. For general information, contact:
Fédération Française de Cyclotourisme Ligue de Bretagne
✉ **10 rue A. Guérin, Rennes**
☎ **02 99 36 38 11**

Equestrian Sports
Brittany has some 2,000km of designated bridlepaths. Lamballe, Huelgoat, Hennebont and Fougères are good places for pony-trekking. You can hire horse-drawn caravans in the Armorique regional park. For a list of riding centres, contact:
Association Régionale de Tourisme Equestre de Bretagne (ARTEB)
✉ **33 rue Laënnec, 29710 Plonéis** ☎ **02 98 91 02 02**

Ligue Equestre de Bretagne
✉ **17 rue 62e RI, 56100 Lorient**
☎ **02 97 84 44 00**

Golf
Brittany currently has 32 courses of great diversity and interest, many in beautiful locations with ocean views. Golfing packages are available through specialist operators. For general information, contact:
Golf de Bretagne
✉ **130 rue Eugéne Pottier, 35000 Rennes** ☎ **02 99 31 68 83**

Dinard
Golf de Dinard
This glamorous links course, the second oldest in France, overlooks one of the most picturesque stretches of the Emerald Coast.

✉ **Boulevard de la Houle, St-Briac-sur-Mer** ☎ **02 99 88 32 07**

Hiking and Rambling
Brittany has over 4,500km of waymarked routes. For more information contact:
Association Bretonne des Relais et Itinéraires (ABRI)
✉ **4 rue Ronsard, 35000 Rennes**
☎ **02 99 26 13 50**

Maison de la Randonnée
✉ **9 rue des Portes-Mordelaises, 35000 Rennes**
☎ **02 99 67 42 21**

Boating
Brittany has around 650km of navigable inland waterways. Dozens of companies hire craft for self-drive boating holidays at many centres around Brittany's canals, rivers, estuaries and lakes.

Comité de Promotion Touristique des Canaux Breton
Information on leisure facilities and boat hire on Brittany's canals.
✉ **Office du Tourisme, place de la Réblique, 35600 Redon**
☎ **02 99 71 06 04**

Comité Regional du Tourisme de Bretagne
Useful tourist publications on inland waterbased activities include *D'Une Rive à l'Autre* and *Bretagne Fluviale*.
✉ **1 rue Raoul Ponchon, 35069 Rennes** ☎ **02 99 36 15 15**

Formules Bretagne
Information on leisure-boat hire and a wide range of boating holidays.
✉ **203 boulevard St-Germain, 75007 Paris** ☎ **01 53 63 11 53**

Sailing

If you want tuition, look for a sailing school with the accreditation *Ecole Française de Voile*.

Centre Nautique de Fouesnant

Long-established sailing school offering tuition and competitions for many different classes of sailing craft; courses for children and young people.

✉ 1 Chemin de Kersentic, Fouesnant ☎ 02 98 56 01 05

Centre Nautique des Glénans

A major training school offering year-round tuition for individuals and groups on dinghies and cruising yachts. Book ahead – courses are generally over-subscribed.

✉ 8 place P Giannay, Concarneau ☎ 02 98 97 14 84

Ecole National de Voile

Based in the sheltered waters east of Quiberon, France's national sailing school is one of Europe's leading centres.

✉ St-Pierre-Quiberon
☎ 02 97 30 30 30

Ligue de Bretagne de Voile

For general information about sailing in Brittany.
✉ 1 rue Kerbriant, BP 39, 29281 Brest ☎ 02 98 02 49 67

Sand–yachting

The Baie de Mont-St-Michel, Pléneuf-Val-André and Plestin-les-Grèves are especially popular for this sport. Look for the EFCV accreditation.

Centre Nautique Municipal EFCV

One of Brittany's largest centres; courses all year; national competitions.

✉ Avenue de la Lieue de Grève, St-Efflam, Plestin-les-Grèves ☎ 02 96 35 62 25

La Ligue de Bretagne Vol Libre

For hang-gliding and 'parapente'.

✉ 147 Plaage St Guirec, 22700 Perros Guirec ☎ 02 96 91 67 50

Noroît Club

Tuition and sand-yacht hire are offered all year round. Championships in August.

✉ Cherrueix ☎ 02 99 48 83 01

Scuba diving

Brittany's clear coastal waters offer excellent conditions for wreck-diving and underwater photography. The 'Plongée Bretagne' (PB) designation at sub-aqua clubs is a sign of quality and high safety standards. For general information, contact:

Comité Interrégional Bretagne–Pays-de-Loire de PSM

✉ 39 rue de la Villeneuve, 56100 Lorient ☎ 02 97 37 51 51

Surfing and Windsurfing

Many clubs teach surfing and provide equipment hire. One of the most exciting places for experienced surfers is the Plage de la Torche, off southern Finistère. Windsurfing is available in many coastal and lake resorts. St-Malo has good facilities.

Ecole de Surf de Bretagne

Longboard and bodyboard tuition in exhilarating Atlantic breakers; can be dangerous in adverse conditions.

✉ Pointe de la Torche, Plomeur ☎ 02 98 58 53 80

Société Nautique de la Baie de St-Malo

✉ Quai du Bajoyer, St-Malo
☎ 02 99 40 11 45

Surf School

✉ 2 avenue de la Hoguette, St-Malo ☎ 02 99 40 07 47

Thalossotherapy

Brittany is one of France's keenest exponents of seawater health cures. Thalassotherapy centres have sprung up in about a dozen resorts, including Bénodet, Carnac, Dinard, Roscoff, Quiberon and St-Malo. You can bask in seawater whirlpools, inhale marine aerosol vapours, be massaged with high-pressure jets and smeared with strange seaweed creams and marine mud – all in the interests of health and beauty. Special spa breaks can be arranged – ask for a brochure from the French Tourist Office or check out www.thalasso.thermes. org.

What's On When

Breton Music Festivals

Traditional Breton music has made a great come-back in recent years, largely the result of successful musicians like Alan Stivell who plays the Celtic harp, and the promotion of the style at major popular events like Lorient's huge Interceltique Festival and Quimper's Festival de Cornouaille. Many smaller celebrations take place, the most typical being a *fest-noz* (night festival) – the Breton equivalent of a Celtic *ceilidh*, with music, storytelling and dancing, and quite a lot of alcohol. A *bagad* is another kind of gathering, when Breton bands assemble to practise their skills on the *bombarde* and the *biniou*. These are advertised locally – ask any tourist office about forthcoming events, or check the Breton music section of the daily newspaper *Ouest-France*.

Most of Brittany's festivals and cultural events take place in the short tourist season between Easter and October. Precise dates may change from year to year. Annually updated events listings are available from regional and local tourist offices.

April

Bécherel: Fête du Livre (books)
Erquy: Fête des Coquilles (scallops)
Perros-Guirec: Cartoon and Comic Festival

May

St-Brieuc: Art Rock Festival
Tréguier: Pardon de St Yves

June

Le Faouët: Pardon de Ste Barbe
Nantes: Quinzaine Celtique
Rumengol: Pardon
St-Jean-du-Doigt: Pardon du Feu

July

Binic: Cod Festival
Dinan: Fête des Remparts (every two years)
Douarnenez: Fêtes des Vieux Gréements (traditional sailing vessels; every two years)
Fouesnant: Fête des Pommiers (apple trees)
Lamballe: Fête des Ajoncs d'Or (gorse flowers)
Locquirec: Pardon de St Jacques/Festival of the Sea
Locronan: Petites/Grandes Troménies (annual/every six years, next festival takes place in 2007)
Morlaix: Wednesday Street Festival
Nantes: International Summer Festival
Pont l'Abbé: Fête des Brodeuses (embroidery)

Quimper: Festival de Cornouaille
Rennes: Tombées de la Nuit
St-Brieuc: Breton Music Festival
Ste-Anne-d'Auray: Grand Pardon
Vannes: Fêtes Historiques (medieval festival)

August

Concarneau: Fête des Filets Bleus (Blue Nets)
Guingamp: Breton Dance and St-Loup Festival
Ile de Fedrun: Fête de la Brière
Lamballe: Fête du Cheval (horses)
Lizio: Festival Artisanal
Lorient: Interceltic Festival
Moncontour: Medieval Fair
Paimpol: Fête du Chant Marin (sea-shanties)
Perros-Guirec: Fête des Hortensias (hydrangeas)
Pont-Aven: Fête des Fleurs d'Ajoncs (gorse flowers)
St-Briac-sur-Mer: Fête des Mouettes (seagulls)
Ste-Anne-la-Palud: Pardon
Vannes: Jazz Festival

September

Camaret: Blessing of the Sea
Carnac: Pardon
Le Folgoët: Grand Pardon
Josselin: Pardon de Notre-Dame-du-Roncier

October

Dinard: British Film Festival
Redon: Fête La Teillouse (chestnut)

November

Brest: Festival du Film Court de Brest (short films)
Nantes: Three Continents Festival (film and cinema)

December

Rennes: Transmusicales (rock festival)

Practical Matters

Above: *Typical Breton motifs used on faience ware unique to Quimper*
Right: *Decorated urn, Château de Caradeuc*

TIME DIFFERENCES

GMT
12 noon

France
→ 1PM

Germany
→ 1PM

USA (NY)
← 7AM

Netherlands
→ 1PM

Spain
→ 1PM

BEFORE YOU GO

WHAT YOU NEED

		UK	Germany	USA	Netherlands	Spain
● Required	Some countries require a passport to remain valid					
○ Suggested	for a minimum period (usually al least six months)					
▲ Not required	beyond the date of entry – contact their consulate or embassy or your travel agent for details.					
Passport/National Identity Card		●	●	●	●	●
Visa (Regulations can change – check before your journey)		▲	▲	▲	▲	▲
Onward or Return Ticket		▲	▲	▲	▲	▲
Health Inoculations		▲	▲	▲	▲	▲
Health Documentation (reciprocal agreement document, ➤ 123, Health)		●	●	●	●	●
Travel Insurance		○	○	○	○	○
Driving Licence (national)		●	●	●	●	●
Car Insurance Certificate (if own car)		○	○	○	○	○
Car Registration Document (if own car)		●	●	●	●	●

WHEN TO GO

Dinard

███████ High season

⬜ Low season

8°C	9°C	12°C	13°C	16°C	18°C	21°C	21°C	18°C	22°C	11°C	9°C
JAN	FEB	MAR	APR	MAY	JUN	JUL	AUG	SEP	OCT	NOV	DEC
🌧	🌧	🌧	⛅	☀	☀	☀	☀	🌧	⛅	🌧	🌧

🌧 Wet   ⛅ Showers   ☀ Sun

TOURIST OFFICES

In the UK
French Tourist Office
178 Piccadilly
London W1V 0AL
☎ 09068 244 123 (60p per minute at all times)
fax 020 7493 6594

Brittany Tourist
Information Point
Crêperie Chez Lindsay
11 Hill Rise,
Richmond
Surrey TW10 6UQ
fax 020 8332 0129

In the USA
French Government
Tourist Office
444 Madison Avenue
New York NY 10022
☎ 212/838 7800
fax 212/838 7855

WHEN YOU ARE THERE

ARRIVING

Airports at Dinard, Brest, Rennes and Nantes take international flights. Ferries travel from the UK to St-Malo and Roscoff, and from Ireland to Roscoff. Shorter crossings to Caen and Cherbourg in Normandy may be cheaper and almost as convenient.

Rennes Airport   Journey times
Kilometres to city centre

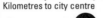

🚇	N/A
6 kilometres 🚌	10 minutes
🚗	10 minutes

Nantes Airport   Journey times
Kilometres to city centre

🚇	N/A
12 kilometres 🚌	20 minutes
🚗	15 minutes

MONEY

The euro is the official currency of France. There are seven euro bank notes (5, 10, 20, 50, 100, 200 and 500 euros), and eight coins (1, 2, 5, 10, 20 and 50 cents, and 1 and 2 euros). Travellers' cheques can be changed at most banks, but take some cash (many banks close on Mondays as well as weekends). Visa/Barclaycard (Carte Bleue) and MasterCard/Access (Eurocard) are widely accepted in hotels, restaurants and major stores.

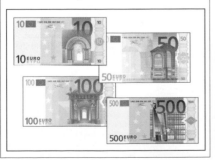

TIME

France is one hour ahead of Greenwich Mean Time (GMT +1), but from late March, when the clocks are put forward one hour, until late October, French summer time (GMT +2) operates.

CUSTOMS

YES

Goods obtained duty free inside the EU or goods bought outside the EU (Limits):
Alcohol (over 22% vol): 1L *or*
Alcohol (not over 22% vol): 2L *and*
Still table wine: 2L
Cigarettes: 200 *or* Cigars: 50 *or* Tobacco: 250gm
Perfume: 60ml
Toilet water: 250ml
Goods bought duty and tax paid for own use inside the EU (Guidance Levels):
Alcohol (over 22% vol): 10L
Alcohol (not over 22% vol): 20L *and* Wine (max 60L sparkling): 90L
Beer: 110L
Cigarettes: 800, Cigars: 200, Tobacco: 1kg
Perfume and Toilet water: no limit

You must be 17 or over to benefit from the alcohol and tobacco allowances.

NO

Drugs, firearms, ammunition, offensive weapons, obscene material, unlicensed animals.

EMBASSIES AND CONSULATES

UK	**Germany**	**USA**	**Netherlands**	**Spain**
01 44 51 31 00	01 53 83 45 00	01 43 12 22 22	01 40 62 33 00	01 44 43 18 00
(Paris)	(Paris)			

WHEN YOU ARE THERE

TOURIST OFFICES

Comité Régional du Tourisme de Bretagne
● 1 rue Raoul Ponchon 35069 Rennes Cedex
☎ 02 99 36 15 15

Departmental Tourist Offices
● Comité Départemental de Tourisme de Finistère
11 rue Théodore Le Hars
29104 Quimper Cedex
☎ 02 98 76 20 70

● Comité Départemental de Tourisme de Côtes d'Amor
7 rue St-Benoît-BP 4620
22046 St-Brieuc
☎ 02 96 62 72 00

● Comité Départemental de Tourisme d'Ille-et-Vilaine
4 rue Jean Jaurès
35000 Rennes
☎ 02 99 78 47 47

● Comité Départemental de Tourisme de Loire-Atlantique
2 allée Baco BP 20502
44005 Nantes Cedex
☎ 02 51 72 95 30

● Comité Départemental de Tourisme de Morbihan
PIBS-Kérino, allée N
Le Blanc
56000 Vannes
☎ 02 97 54 06 56

NATIONAL HOLIDAYS

J	F	M	A	M	J	J	A	S	O	N	D
1		(2)	(2)	3(2)	(2)	1	1			2	1

1 Jan	New Year's Day
Mar/Apr	Easter Sunday and Monday
1 May	Labour Day
8 May	VE Day
May	Ascension Day
May/Jun	Whit Sunday and Monday
14 Jul	Bastille Day
15 Aug	Assumption Day
1 Nov	All Saints' Day
11 Nov	Remembrance Day
25 Dec	Christmas Day

OPENING HOURS

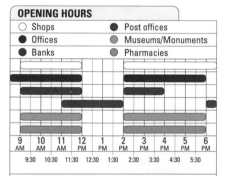

In addition to the times shown above, afternoon times of shops in summer can extend in the most popular centres. Most shops close Sunday and many on Monday. Small food shops open from 7AM and may open Sunday morning.
Large department stores do not close for lunch and hypermarkets open 10AM to 9 or 10PM, but may shut Monday morning.
Banks are closed Sunday as well as Saturday or Monday.
Many post offices are open until 8PM.
Museums and monuments have extended summer hours. Many close one day a week: either Monday (municipal ones) or Tuesday (national ones).

DRIVE ON THE
RIGHT

TOILETS
FREE

PUBLIC TRANSPORT

A free guide called *Guide-Envie* summarises all public transport networks in Brittany, and is available at tourist offices.

Internal Flights Regular flights from Paris and other French cities with Air France to Nantes, Rennes, Brest, Lannion, Lorient, Quimper (just over 1 hour). BritAir (subsidiary of Air France) operates daily flights between Nantes and Brest. Finis'Air connects Brest and the Ile d'Ouessant.

Trains Fast TGV trains connect Paris with Nantes, Rennes, Lorient, Quimper and Brest. Within Brittany, SNCF rail lines run from Rennes along the north and south coasts, but there are few cross-country routes.

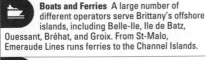

Buses Most major towns have a bus station (*gare routière*), but the bus network is fragmented and many different companies operate. The coast has more regular routes than the interior. Some services run in conjunction with the railway (SNCF). Many timetables are designed to serve the needs of commuters and schoolchildren; services are dramatically reduced at weekends.

Boats and Ferries A large number of different operators serve Brittany's offshore islands, including Belle-Ile, Ile de Batz, Ouessant, Bréhat, and Groix. From St-Malo, Emeraude Lines runs ferries to the Channel Islands.

Urban Transport Major centres have urban bus services. Rennes has a limited metro service, mainly used by commuters. Nantes has an extensive, well-integrated and very efficient mass transit network, including trams. Tourist passes are available.

CAR RENTAL

All large towns have car-rental agencies at their airports and railway stations. Car hire is expensive, but airlines and tour operators offer fly-drive and French Railways (SNCF) train-car packages, often more economical than hiring locally.

TAXIS

Taxis are a costlier option than public transport. They pick up at taxi ranks (*stations de taxi*) found at railway stations and airports. Hotels and restaurants can usually give a taxi call number. Check the taxi has a meter; there is a pick-up charge plus a rate per minute.

DRIVING

Speed limits on toll motorways (autoroutes): **130kph** (**110kph** when wet); non-toll motorways and dual carriageways: **110kph** (**100kph** when wet). In fog (visibility less than 50m): **50kph** all roads

Speed limits on country roads: **90kph** (**80kph** when wet)

Speed limits on urban roads: **50kph** (limit starts at town sign)

Must be worn in front seats at all times and in rear seats where fitted.

Random breath-testing. Never drive under the influence of alcohol

Petrol (*essence*) including unleaded (*sans plomb*), and diesel (*gasoil*) is widely available. Petrol stations are numerous along main roads but rarer in rural areas. Some on minor roads are closed on Sundays. Maps showing petrol stations are available from main tourist offices.

A red warning triangle must be carried if your car has no hazard warning lights. Place the triangle 30m behind the car in the event of an accident or breakdown. On motorways ring from emergency phones (every 2km) to contact the breakdown service. Off motorways, police will advise on local breakdown services.

PERSONAL SAFETY

The *Police Municipale* (blue uniforms) carry out police duties in cities and towns. The *Gendarmes* (blue trousers, black jackets, white belts), the national police force, cover the countryside and smaller places. The *CRS* deal with emergencies and also look after safety on beaches.

To avoid danger or theft:
• Do not use unmanned roadside rest areas at night.
• Cars, especially foreign cars, should be secured.
• In crowded places, beware of pickpockets.

Police assistance:
☎ **17**
from any call box

TELEPHONES

Telephone numbers in France comprise ten digits; the first two numbers for Brittany are 02 (omit 0 if dialling from the UK). Nearly all public phones use pre-paid cards now (*télécartes*). Currently these cost 7.50 and 15 euros respectively at post offices, tobacconists and branches of France Télécom. Some cards give cheaper overseas calls than

standard *télécartes*, so ask before you buy if you need to phone abroad. You need to dial the international code if you're phoning abroad with a mobile.

International Dialling Codes From France:	
UK:	00 44
Germany:	00 49
USA & Canada:	00 1
Netherlands:	00 31
Spain:	00 34

POST

The PTT (*Postes et Télécommunications*) deals with mail and telephone services. Outside main centres, post offices open shorter hours and may close 12–2. Letter boxes are yellow. Open: 8AM–7PM (12 Sat). Closed: Sun. Main post office in Rennes: place de la République; in Nantes: place de Bretagne.

ELECTRICITY

The French power supply is: 220 volts
Type of socket:

Round two-hole sockets taking two-round-pin (or occasionally three-round-pin) plugs. British visitors should bring an adaptor; US visitors a voltage transformer.

TIPS/GRATUITIES

	Yes ✓ No ✗	
Restaurants (service incl, tip optional)	✗	
Cafés/Bar (service incl, tip optional)	✗	
Hotels (service incl, tip optional	✗	
Hairdressers	✓	€1–1.50
Taxis	✓	€1–1.50
Tour guides	✓	€1–1.50
Cinema usherettes	✓	€1–1.50
Cloakroom attendants	✓	small
Toilet attendants	✓	small

What to photograph: the coast, with its reefs, rocks and islands; parish closes and calvaries; standing stones; rural villages and timber-framed houses; abbey and château ruins; Fougères castle.
Restrictions: some museums will allow you to photograph inside. In churches with frescoes and icons, prior permission is required for flashlight.
Where to buy film: the most popular brands and types of film can be bought from shops and photo laboratories. Film development is quite expensive.

HEALTH

Insurance
Nationals of EU and certain other countries can get medical treatment in France at reduced cost on production of a qualifying form (Form E111 for Britons), although private medical insurance is still advised and is essential for all other visitors.

Dental Services
As for general medical treatment (see above, **Insurance**), nationals of EU countries can obtain dental treatment at reduced cost. About 70 per cent of a dentist's standard fee can be refunded. Private medical insurance is still advisable for all.

Sun Advice
The sunniest (and hottest) months are July and August, but the good weather can start in June and continue to October. Generally the weather is relatively mild, though take care on the beach and when walking. Drink plenty of fluids, wear a hat and make sure you apply a good sunscreen.

Drugs
Pharmacies – recognised by their green cross sign – have qualified staff able to offer medical advice, provide first aid and prescribe and provide a wide range of drugs, though some are available by prescription (*ordonnance*) only.

Safe Water
It is safe to drink tap water served in hotels and restaurants, but never drink from a tap marked *eau non potable* (not drinking water). Many prefer the taste of bottled water, which is cheap and widely available.

CONCESSIONS

Students/Youths A youth card (*Carte Jeune*), available to those under 26, entitles holders to various discounts on public transport, museum admissions, entertainments, shopping and other facilities (including meals in university canteens): ask at tourist offices and post offices for details.

Senior Citizens A number of tour companies offer special arrangements for senior citizens; for further information contact the French Tourist Office (► 118, **Tourist Offices**). Senior citizens (aged over 60) are eligible for reduced or free entrance to sights, and (aged over 65) fare discounts on public transport.

CLOTHING SIZES

France	UK	Rest of Europe	USA		
46	36	46	36		
48	38	48	38		
50	40	50	40		
52	42	52	42		Suits
54	44	54	44		
56	46	56	46		
41	7	41	8		
42	7½	42	8½		
43	8½	43	9½		
44	9½	44	10½		Shoes
45	10½	45	11½		
46	11	46	12		
37	14½	37	14½		
38	15	38	15		
39/40	15½	39/40	15½		
41	16	41	16		Shirts
42	16½	42	16½		
43	17	43	17		
36	8	34	6		
38	10	36	8		
40	12	38	10		
42	14	40	12		Dresses
44	16	42	14		
46	18	44	16		
38	4½	38	6		
38	5	38	6½		
39	5½	39	7		
39	6	39	7½		Shoes
40	6½	40	8		
41	7	41	8½		

WHEN DEPARTING

● Remember to contact the airport on the day before leaving to ensure the flight details are unchanged.

● If travelling by ferry you must check in no later than the time specified on your ticket.

● Check the duty-free limits of the country you are entering before departure.

LANGUAGE

French is the native language. English is spoken widely, especially by those involved in the tourist trade and working in the larger and most popular centres; in smaller, rural places fewer people speak English. In any case, attempts to speak French, or at least to greet others in French, will be much appreciated. Below is a list of helpful words. More extensive coverage can be found in the AA's *Essential French Phrase Book*.

🛏	hotel	*l'hôtel*	rate	*le tarif*
	guest house	*chambre d'hôte*	breakfast	*le petit déjeuner*
	room	*la chambre*	toilet	*les toilettes*
	single room	*une personne*	bathroom	*la salle de bain*
	double room	*deux personnes*	shower	*la douche*
	per person	*par personne*	balcony	*le balcon*
	per room	*par chambre*	key	*la clef/clé*
	one/two nights	*une/deux nuits*	chambermaid	*femme*
	reservation	*la réservation*		*de chambre*
🪙	bank	*la banque*	banknote	*le billet*
	exchange office	*le bureau de*	coin	*la pièce*
		change	credit card	*la carte de*
	post office	*la poste*		*crédit*
	cashier	*le caissier*	travellers'	*le chèque de*
	foreign	*le change*	cheque	*voyage*
	exchange	*extérieur*	exchange rate	*le taux de*
	English pound	*la livre sterling*		*change*
🍴	restaurant	*la restaurant*	starter	*le hors d'œuvre*
	café	*le café*	main course	*le plat principal*
	table	*la table*	dish of the day	*le plat du jour*
	menu	*le menu*	dessert	*le dessert*
	set menu	*le menu du jour*	drink	*la boisson*
	wine list	*la carte des vins*	waiter	*le garçon*
	lunch	*le déjeuner*	waitress	*la serveuse*
	dinner	*le dîner*	the bill	*l'addition*
🚌	aeroplane	*l'avion*	single/return	*simple/retour*
	airport	*l'aéroport*	ticket office	*le guichet*
	train	*le train*	timetable	*l'horaire*
	train station	*la gare*	seat	*la place*
	bus	*l'autobus*	first class	*première classe*
	bus station	*la gare routière*	second class	*seconde classe*
	ferry/boat	*le bateau*	non-smoking	*non-fumeurs*
	port	*le port*	reserved	*réservé*
	ticket	*le billet*	window	*la fenêtre*
💬	yes	*oui*	today	*aujourd'hui*
	no	*non*	tomorrow	*demain*
	please	*s'il vous plaît*	yesterday	*hier*
	thank you	*merci*	how much?	*combien?*
	hello	*bonjour*	expensive	*cher*
	goodbye	*au revoir*	open	*ouvert*
	goodnight	*bonsoir*	closed	*fermé*
	sorry	*pardon*	you're welcome	*de rien*
	excuse me	*excusez-moi*	okay	*d'accord*
	help!	*au secours!*	I don't know	*je ne sais pas*

INDEX

Acknowledgements
The Automobile Association would like to thank the following photographers and libraries for their assistance in the preparation of this book.

WORLD PICTURES 80, 84; **www.euro.ecb.int** 119 (euros)

The remaining photographs are held in the Association's own library (AA PHOTO LIBRARY) and were taken by Rick Strange, with the exception of the following:
ADRIAN BAKER Front Cover d (seafood), 5b, 6b, 8b, 24b, 30, 33, 34t, 35t, 36, 37t, 38, 40t, 41t, 44, 48c, 82/83, 90; STEVE DAY 5t, 6t, 7t, 7b, 8t, 9t, 10t, 11t, 12t, 13t, 14t, 14ct, 14c, 18b, 19c, 25c, 42, 45, 46b, 54, 55, 56, 57, 58t, 58c, 59t, 59c, 60t, 60c, 63, 64t, 64b, 65t, 65c, 66, 67t, 73c, 117b; J EDMANSON 69, 70t, 72t, 73t, 74t, 75t, 78t, 79, 122l ; PAUL KENWARD Front Cover a (Creperie Sign), 78b, 122t; RICH NEWTON 13t, 13c; T OLIVER 122r; CLIVE SAWYER 67b; MICHAEL SHORT 46c; BARRIE SMITH Front Cover h (Antrain, Château) 21b, 27t, 21, 70b, 117tl, 117tr; ROY VICTOR Front Cover background (Rennes, buildings), 8c, 9ct, 12b, 15t, 16t, 17t, 18t, 19t, 20t, 21t, 22t, 23t, 24t, 25t, 26t, 27b, 41c, 47, 51b, 61c, 85b.

Revision Management: Apostrophe S Limited

Dear Essential Traveller

Your comments, opinions and recommendations are very important to us. So please help us to improve our travel guides by taking a few minutes to complete this simple questionnaire.

You do not need a stamp (unless posted outside the UK). If you do not want to cut this page from your guide, then photocopy it or write your answers on a plain sheet of paper.

Send to: **The Editor, AA World Travel Guides, FREEPOST SCE 4598, Basingstoke RG21 4GY.**

Your recommendations...

We always encourage readers' recommendations for restaurants, nightlife or shopping – if your recommendation is used in the next edition of the guide, we will send you a *FREE* AA *Essential* **Guide** of your choice. Please state below the establishment name, location and your reasons for recommending it.

_____

_____

_____

_____

Please send me **AA *Essential*** _____

About this guide...

Which title did you buy?
   AA *Essential* _____
Where did you buy it? _____
When? m m / y y

Why did you choose an AA *Essential* Guide? _____

_____

_____

_____

_____

Did this guide meet your expectations?
   Exceeded ☐   Met all ☐   Met most ☐   Fell below ☐
   Please give your reasons _____

_____

_____

_____

continued on next page...

Were there any aspects of this guide that you particularly liked? _____

_____

_____

Is there anything we could have done better? _____

_____

_____

About you...

Name (*Mr/Mrs/Ms*) _____

Address _____

_____

_____ Postcode _____

Daytime tel nos _____

Please only give us your mobile phone number if you wish to hear from us about other products and services from the AA and partners by text or mms.

Which age group are you in?
Under 25 ☐   25–34 ☐   35–44 ☐   45–54 ☐   55–64 ☐   65+ ☐

How many trips do you make a year?
Less than one ☐   One ☐   Two ☐   Three or more ☐

Are you an AA member? Yes ☐   No ☐

About your trip...

When did you book? m m / y y   When did you travel? m m / y y

How long did you stay? _____

Was it for business or leisure? _____

Did you buy any other travel guides for your trip?

If yes, which ones? _____

Thank you for taking the time to complete this questionnaire. Please send it to us as soon as possible, and remember, you do not need a stamp (*unless posted outside the UK*).

Happy Holidays!

The Atlas

Acknowledgements
All pictures are from AA World Travel Library with contributions from the following photographers:
Roy Victor: paragliding at Menez-Hom, ruins of Forteresse de Largoet
Alex Kouprianoff: exterior of house in Rennes, Pointe du Raz
Paul Kenward: medieval fête in Moncontour

The Automobile Association
www.theAA.com
The Automobile Association's website offers comprehensive and up-to-the-minute information covering AA-approved hotels, guest houses and B&Bs, restaurants and pubs in the UK; airport parking, insurance, European breakdown cover, European motoring advice, a ferry planner, European route planner, overseas fuel prices, a bookshop and much more.

The Foreign and Commonwealth Office
Country advice, traveller's tips, before you go information, checklists and more.
www.fco.gov.uk

GENERAL

UK Passport Service
www.ukpa.gov.uk

Health Advice for Travellers
www.doh.gov.uk/traveladvice

BBC – Holiday
www.bbc.co.uk/holiday

The Full Universal Currency Converter
www.xe.com/ucc/full.shtml

Flying with Kids
www.flyingwithkids.com

Covers Haute Bretagne. Very visual with good photographs and two virtual tours of the region. English version.
www.bretagne35.com

Official department site. In French only. Lacking in pictures, but the essentials are there.
www.finisteretourisme.com

Extensive choice of languages. Detailed site including two videos. Good section on contemporary artists of the region.
www.tourismebretagne.com

Official site for the city of Rennes. Lots of information regarding the daily events in the city, also has a virtual tour.
www.ville-rennes.fr

In French, English, Spanish, Italian and German. Good for shopping, museums, monuments and sport. Practical, with city centre maps and a section 'Nantes kids'.
www.nantes-tourisme.com

In both French and English. Good photographs and detailed practical information on the sites and monuments.
www.saint-malo-tourisme.com

Good selection of self-catering accommo-dation – houses, gîtes and appartments.
www.homelidays.com

Good reading, lots of historical background, visually attractive. Lacks a little in practical information. French only.
www.cotesdarmor.com

Good content. Historical information, places to visit, walks and tours. Themed short stays, such as boating or fishing, and weekend breaks. In French only.
www.morbihan.com

Very practical, lots of historical information and strong on hotel recommendations and reservations. In French only.
www.brest-france.com

Cultural festivals with contact details and calendar of events. French only.
www.gouelioubreizh.com

TRAVEL

www.cheapflights.co.uk
www.thisistravel.co.uk
www.ba.com
www.worldairportguide.com

www.britanny-ferries.co.uk
www.poferries.com

le Mans-Est — Motorway with junction
Autobahn mit Anschlussstelle

Date, Datum — Motorway under construction
Autobahn in Bau

Date, Datum — Motorway projected
Autobahn in Planung

® Roadside restaurant and hotel
Raststätte mit
Übernachtungsmöglichkeit

® Roadside restaurant
Raststätte ohne
Übernachtungsmöglichkeit

© Snack bar, kiosk
Erfrischungsstelle, Kiosk

® Ⓐ Filling station, Truck stop
Tankstelle, Autohof

Dual carriageway with
motorway characteristics
with junction
Autobahnähnliche Schnell-
straße mit Anschlussstelle

Dual carriageway
Straße mit zwei
getrennten Fahrbahnen

Thoroughfare
Durchgangsstraße

Important main road
Wichtige Hauptstraße

Main road
Hauptstraße

Other road
Sonstige Straße

Main line railway
Fernverkehrsbahn

Mountain railway
Bergbahn

Car ferry
Autofähre

Route with
beautiful scenery
Landschaftlich besonders
schöne Strecke

*Routes
des Crêtes* — Tourist route
Touristenstraße

Toll road
Straße gegen Gebühr befahrbar

X — X — X Road closed
to motor traffic
Straße für Kraftfahrzeuge
gesperrt

+|+|+|+ Temporarily regulated traffic
Zeitlich geregelter Verkehr

◄ 15% Important gradients
Bedeutende Steigungen

Culture
Kultur

★★ **PARIS**
★★ *la Alhambra*
Worth a journey
Eine Reise wert

★ **TRENTO**
★ *Comburg*
Worth a detour
Lohnt einen Umweg

Landscape
Landschaft

★★ **Rodos**
★★ *Fingal's cave*
Worth a journey
Eine Reise wert

★ **Korab**
★ *Jaskinia raj*
Worth a detour
Lohnt einen Umweg

☀ ᴠ Important panoramic view
Besonders schöner Ausblick

National park, nature park
Nationalpark, Naturpark

4807 ▲ Mountain summit with height
in metres
Bergspitze mit Höhenangabe
in Metern

(630) Elevation
Ortshöhe

♦ Church
Kirche

♦ Church ruin
Kirchenruine

♦ Monastery
Kloster

♦ Monastery ruin
Klosterruine

♦ Palace, castle
Schloss, Burg

♦ Palace ruin, castle ruin
Schloss-, Burgruine

♦ Monument
Denkmal

✓ Waterfall
Wasserfall

∩ Cave
Höhle

∴ Ruins
Ruinenstätte

▪ Other object
Sonstiges Objekt

⋏ Camping site
Campingplatz

✈ Airport
Verkehrsflughafen

⊕ ⊕ Regional airport · Airfield
Regionalflughafen · Flugplatz

```
0          15          30 km
0          10          20 miles
```

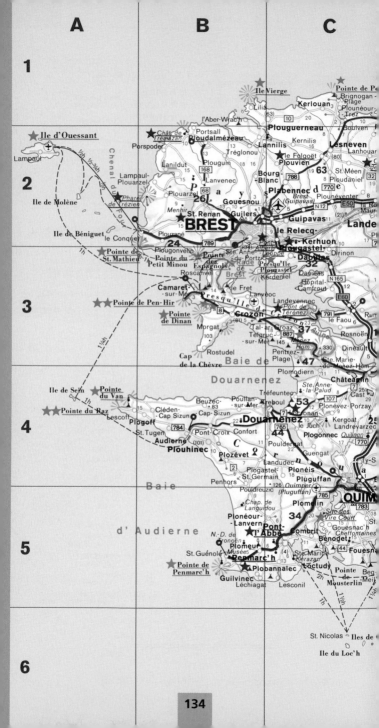

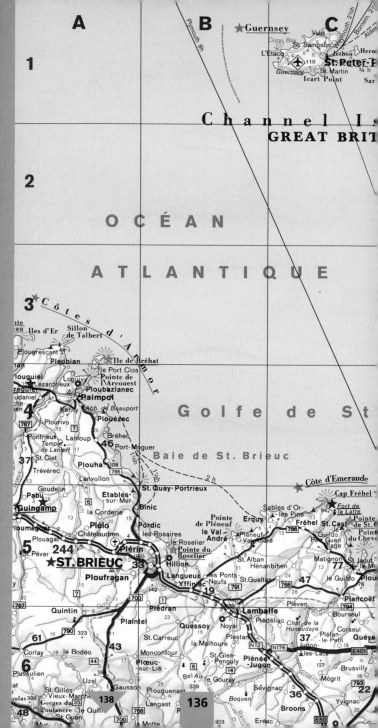

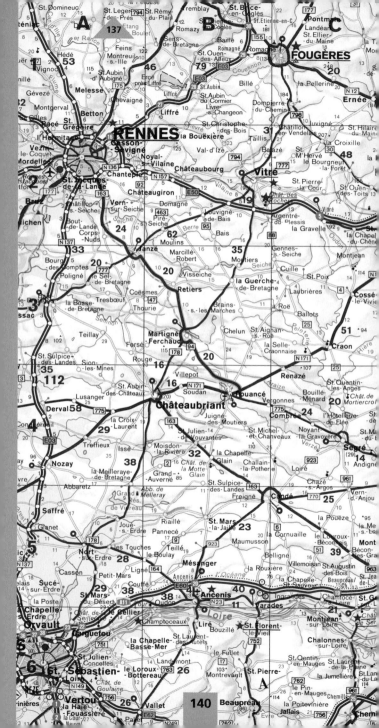

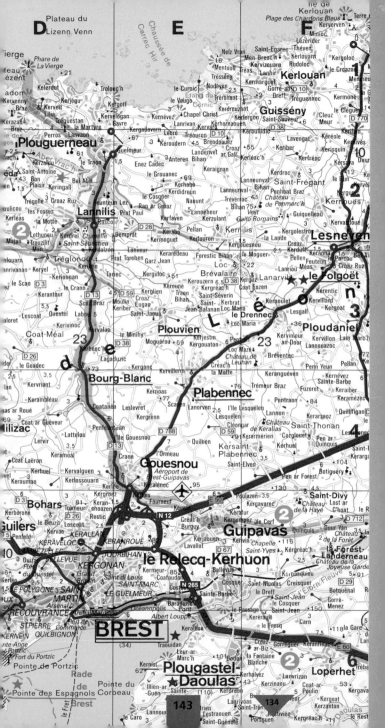

Sight Locator Index

This index relates to the atlas section on pages 134–143. We have given map references to the main sights of interest in the book. Some sights in the index may not be plotted on the atlas. **Note: ibc – inside back cover**

For the main index see pages 125–126